402 Avalon

402 Avalon

Ben Campbell

Copyright © 2015 by Ben Campbell
All rights reserved

Pants-On-Fire Publications
402 Avalon
ISBN-13: 978-1490569161 Paperback
ASIN: B00EXAWVK0 eBook
First Edition

Printed in the United States

License Notes:
All rights are reserved for this memoir under the International and Pan-American Copyright Conventions. Part of this story may be reproduced or transmitted in any form or by any means, electronic or mechanical, including photocopying, recording, or by any information storage and retrieval system, with permission from Ben Campbell.

Photos

Photos of the Campbell family and San Francisco included in this memoir are complimentary visuals. Most photos were taken by members of the Campbell family.

Follow-up:
I have assembled a black and white *MinAleta Campbell Family Photo Album* in eBook and paperback editions as a follow-up to this memoir. Many of the photos in this memoir are included in that photo album, as well as photos of San Francisco from the 1950s. The details are below.

MinAleta Campbell: Family Photo Album
ISBN-13: 978-1490940915 Paperback
ASIN: B00ESQIAYU eBook

Disclosure

This story as told by me, the youngest of six children, is not about Old Mother Goose or The House that Jack Built, and it's not reflective of the personalities, opinions or attitudes of my family members, or of my friends or neighbors, or any other person associated or described in my loose childhood memoir. The events in this narrative are how I had experienced them. This is the story of what some of my family life was like when I was ten and eleven years old while living at 402 Avalon Avenue, San Francisco, California.

I've written this memoir to enhance selected charms and fashions of the 1950s. This memoir is my delayed adulthood take about my idealistic longing for living a brilliant childhood before the computerized world and high-tech devices were invented.

Dedication
For Mom & Dad

I dedicate this memoir to my mom MinAleta and to my dad Albert, to my sister Karen (Campbell) Caudill and her three daughters Deborah Woodward, Sharon Woodward and Kelly Chapple, to my brother Tim Campbell, his wife Margareta and their two children Eva Derksen and Kyle Campbell, to my sister Joyce (Campbell) Peltier, her husband Lee and their two children Leander Peltier and Mark Peltier, and to my brother Ron Campbell who didn't have children but instead raised dozens of flocks of pigeons.

A special dedication goes to our son Corbett, his wife Kristin and our granddaughter Ellery, who perhaps will enjoy reading this memoir about one year in the life of granddaddy Ben.

Photos

Photos of the Campbell family and San Francisco included in this memoir are complimentary visuals. Most photos were taken by members of the Campbell family.

Follow-up:
I have assembled a black and white *MinAleta Campbell Family Photo Album* in eBook and paperback editions as a follow-up to this memoir. Many of the photos in this memoir are included in that photo album, as well as photos of San Francisco from the 1950s. The details are below.

MinAleta Campbell: Family Photo Album
ISBN-13: 978-1490940915 Paperback
ASIN: B00ESQIAYU eBook

Disclosure

This story as told by me, the youngest of six children, is not about Old Mother Goose or The House that Jack Built, and it's not reflective of the personalities, opinions or attitudes of my family members, or of my friends or neighbors, or any other person associated or described in my loose childhood memoir. The events in this narrative are how I had experienced them. This is the story of what some of my family life was like when I was ten and eleven years old while living at 402 Avalon Avenue, San Francisco, California.

I've written this memoir to enhance selected charms and fashions of the 1950s. This memoir is my delayed adulthood take about my idealistic longing for living a brilliant childhood before the computerized world and high-tech devices were invented.

Dedication
For Mom & Dad

I dedicate this memoir to my mom MinAleta and to my dad Albert, to my sister Karen (Campbell) Caudill and her three daughters Deborah Woodward, Sharon Woodward and Kelly Chapple, to my brother Tim Campbell, his wife Margareta and their two children Eva Derksen and Kyle Campbell, to my sister Joyce (Campbell) Peltier, her husband Lee and their two children Leander Peltier and Mark Peltier, and to my brother Ron Campbell who didn't have children but instead raised dozens of flocks of pigeons.

A special dedication goes to our son Corbett, his wife Kristin and our granddaughter Ellery, who perhaps will enjoy reading this memoir about one year in the life of granddaddy Ben.

Preface

ACTIVITIES IN the Campbell family between the years 1950 and 1956, concerning my parents and siblings and friends and neighbors were rich yet bittersweet, rowdy yet peaceful, deft and delightful and attuned with the times.

The animated movie *Hotel Transylvania* is one example what life was like at 402 Avalon. When gears shifted and changes took place in the family around 1955, I'd turned into a quiet introspective boy, a child neglected and disregarded by my parents.

Not because of being ignored but because of wanting guidance, I'd pretended to communicate with spirits that my family members believed inhabited our house.

Evidence that I needed supervision during my youth was continuous. Playing with knives and fire and chasing cars down the street wasn't normal. I wanted answers for my particular anxieties. Why couldn't I be a wooden boy like Pinocchio and not hurt or bleed from cuts?

You can't be a wooden boy, mom told me.

Then I want to be Superman and fly, I said.

That's impossible. Superman is a comic book and people can't fly, she said.

Then I want to be like the mighty robot Gort in *The Day the Earth Stood Still*.

You have to understand, Benny, that Gort isn't real and robots aren't real, mom said. *The Day the Earth Stood Still* is a science fiction movie and it's not real.

I grabbed my toy dump truck and ran outside to play in the empty lot across the street from our house. Why wasn't impossible, possible, I thought. I can be wooden if I want to or fly if I want and even be a robot. Nothing was impossible for me.

When arguments between family members split into crazy disruptive parts I'd go explore the mysteries of time in the garage with the spirits. Family members thought that I was just talking to myself. Little did they know? Supervision wasn't analogous to finding focus, which I needed the most, thus, as the youngest child I was happy playing alone when I was a little urchin, pretending I could fly and really talk to ghosts.

Mom and dad had purpose and they had allusions that something enormous was always about to happen, something majestic like finding a million dollars buried under the house or finding a pirate's chest filled with gold coins in the attic, anything that would elevate the financial status of the Campbell family that lived in the Excelsior District, inside the big wooden dilapidated house at 402 Avalon Avenue.

That huge, frightening three-story wooden house I knew was ready to collapse any day or night into a pile of garbage with us buried underneath it. The constant groaning and rasping in the walls of the house warned me that disaster was imminent in the middle of the night after sleep had claimed us, and we wouldn't even know we had died.

Built on a slight grade, the downside garage was dug into the hillside and could house four cars. The area was enclosed with an eight-foot-high fence with a garage door in it beside the sidewalk that opened inward. One regular size door was beside the garage door in the fence that led to an outside stairwell up to a narrow wooden walkway. Our home was surrounded by a community of smaller 1940s wooden and stiff stucco houses, typically San Francisco architecture, which earmarked the beginning of modern box-type housing tracks.

Since cell phones, personal computers and the Internet were yet to be invented, rumors spread by word of mouth and telephone throughout the decades that 402 Avalon had transformed from the Brown cattle farm into a God-forbidden brothel during the 1920s and then into a damned smelly apartment complex during the 1940s. We settled into the timeworn farmhouse around 1950, much to my surprise and delight.

Old and musty smelling, for the next six years the Campbell family walked on faded and chipped linoleum floors and inhaled rotted and moldy wood odors, all the while engaging and embracing the big city of San Francisco. My family blossomed and not without emotional wrestling in the earmarked rundown house. We clashed and toiled and played as an uneasy, ghost-ridden feel drifted about the building.

The farm house was constructed to tolerate moderate California weather, but surviving California earthquakes was altogether different. The forgiving configuration survived earthquakes while we lived inside, performing daily chores, watching television shows, playing card games and listening to music. Day and night, we listened to the creaking floors and the groaning walls that shifted from small undetected earthquakes that I knew were caused by ghosts.

The friendly spirits occupied the air inside the house, I'd felt their presence by way of inherent moods, but didn't detect visions of anything ghostly. I understood that time abandoned their bodies and their souls endured encroachments from other people living at 402 Avalon. It's as if they owned the property and all new landlords were their guests.

The house was stabilized underneath on cinder pier blocks with ten-foot-tall posts attached to a joist system of beams. When I went to play in the garage-basement by myself warm moods blanketed me. My imagination was escalating into an ocean of assurance that the titanic farmhouse would never implode on top of me. If the house fell down, I'd be a member of the ghost family.

My house was sturdy and I loved playing in the hard dirt the house was built on. The splintered light from one overhead light bulb hanging from a beam spewed down upon me. I played by myself with my toy dump truck and miniature plastic army soldiers, making small roads around mounds of dirt, pretending the soldiers had won the Korean War and I was driving soldiers home in the bed of the dump truck.

I loved digging in the dirt under the house with dad's screwdriver searching for treasure. My head pulsated like a heartbeat when I'd dig. My hand would rise and fall, the journey would last seconds. The screwdriver was guided with splashes of heat from my hands and would strike into the dirt, twist and expose buried quarters, dims and nickels. I'd smile knowing that the coins were gifted to me, guided by something unknown amidst this historic old building.

The house was filled with secrets dead to the world, secrets that inhabitants whispered to themselves, surprises that would never shock anybody again, riddles that would never be solved, mysteries and anomalies that were also dead to the world. I longed to hear the secrets and to acknowledge the surprises and solve the riddles and experience the mysteries and anomalies for myself, but I was ten years old going on eleven, and what would a kid know about such nonsense.

Where I played around the house my bones and skin would warm up, I'd smile and my mind would tell me that I was a guest in the house of intelligent hosts.

If nonsense was real, then why was my family living at 402 Avalon? The outdated farmhouse was now an apartment complex owned by my parents that was built during the 1880s. The looming structure should have been demolished and five or six new houses could have been constructed where five or six families could have flourished inside them.

Why were we living in this spirit occupied structure? I was a progressive thinker and understood that time would answer that question.

402 Avalon Avenue 1956

Campbell Family Oroville Reflections

FROM THE living room window at 402 Avalon, the view of the upper-half of the giant cross on Mt. Davidson across the valley full of row houses was remarkable. Every night the cross was highlighted with lights at ground level and floated like an angel above the treetops.

The forever busy Mission Street was two city-blocks below us where the delicious fragrant doughnut bakery sold its wares. To the left Mission Street hurried to Daly City, to the right the wide street sped to Market Street downtown. The fashionable Granada Theater where I went to see science fiction movies and cartoons was on Mission Street six city-blocks away from Avalon Avenue. Ocean Avenue, the road that drifted toward Playland at-the-Beach was down the street from the Granada Theater.

MinAleta, five children & Missy
1953 Oroville, California

Although the City was approximately 45 square miles, we had easy access to every spectacular corner. San Francisco was a Cosmopolitan City; the Queen of the Pacific, the City by the

Golden Gate, and the City of Many Wonders where the roads to serendipity were paved with good intentions.

My oldest brother, Ronald Leroy Campbell, attended SF City College studying cultural anthropology. My oldest sister, Joyce Marie Campbell, did whatever she wanted to do. My other brother, Timothy Edwin Campbell, and sister, Karen Yvonne Campbell and I, Albert Benjamin Campbell, formed an informal pre-teen and teenage gang, and missy our dog was our expressive mascot pooch.

Our parents owned summer shack sixty-eight miles north of Sacramento in God-forsaken, oak tree harassed Oroville, California, where my mother felt that the festering summer heat helped dull her rheumatoid arthritis pain. This is funny. The shanty's kitchen had a sink with a well pump-head that consisted of a spigot and pumping arm. The well was dry so when we spent summers there, getting water was synonymous to survival. How about a telephone? No, we didn't have a telephone either. Hmmm, we had no water and no telephone. What if an emergency occurred? Did we have electricity? Oh yeah, we had electricity but no television. On dark nights with strong winds rattling the windows, we'd settle in and listen to *The Shadow* radio program, a crime-fighting vigilante with psychic powers posing as a wealthy, young man about town. The radio program always started with a menacing voice: *Who knows what evil lurks in the hearts of men?* Those words were accompanied by an ominous laugh and the musical theme, *Camille Saint-Saëns' Le Rouet d'Omphale*.

Did we have a bathroom inside our shack? No, we didn't. We had a smelly, spider and green-horse-fly ridden outhouse in the front yard fifty feet from the house. I was scared to death of the smelly pit on stormy nights, carrying a flashlight with wind and rain crashing against my little body, my little wet feet stepping in muddy puddles, my tiny hands swinging the wooden door open on rusty hinges, where dozens of frogs croaked and eyes glowed from my flashlight. Edgar Allan Poe must have experienced the same with his outhouse in mind when he wrote the first line to his poem **The Raven**: *Once upon a midnight dreary, while I pondered, weak and weary.*

Our outhouse wasn't a *Stop and Smell the Roses* potty, the

hell-hole was a *somewhere a village is missing its morgue*. I didn't want to use the hair-raising latrine because of the deadly aroma, but the alternative of getting a tick lodged up my butt, or if I scurried behind a bush poison ivy would invade my crotch. Can you tell that I didn't love the outhouse? With all good intension, pooping and peeing anywhere on the property, out in the open, even in the rain, was better than sitting on the seat above the pit toilet.

Back row from left: Bobby Elliot, Karen, MinAleta sitting.
Front row from left: Timmy, Jackie Elliot, Benny, Joyce 1954

I called our Oroville property insomnia, a word I'd learned from my mom, because mosquitos were hell-bent biting me and keeping me awake. We stayed in Oroville at least six weeks during summer school breaks. I couldn't hate the scorching weather any more than I hated buzzing mosquitos and wasps that were a constant courtesy of nature. The redeeming value in that, *the wheel is turning, but the hamster is dead* place, was that we could swim in Feather River near downtown Oroville. The concrete diving platform that was at least ten feet above the swift river currents, always tempted me, but I was smart enough not to jump off and slam my little body into the icy water. Good thing I was the sharpest knife in the drawer between the ages of five and ten when we stayed those summers in Oroville, otherwise I'd have been another child victim drowned in the deep Feather River.

Hanging out at the Feather River Park with unforgiving swarms of mosquitos, hungry ticks, killer spiders, stinky skunks, ratty raccoons, devilish dragonflies and fire-breathing dragon heat, all the creepy factors haunted the town of Oroville. One good feature about the environment were the colorful dragonflies eating flies, bees, ants and wasps, but they were outnumbered and ill-equipped against the throng of local predators, as well as they couldn't think their way out of a paper bag.

Timmy, Karen, Benny
Feather River, Oroville, CA 1952

The park was also a treat for young families picnicking and a hangout for teenagers connecting. Whenever we frequented Feather River Park I'd observe the social life of teens and wonder if I'd ever experience kissing a girl behind a tree or chase and tackle one on the grass. That madness was for my older sister Joyce and older brother Ronnie, but not for me.

Our hovel in the searing heat, which mom loved, was the junket of deception, a place to dwell rather than grow in those days. The heat and insects were so intense and threatening and the dislocation and up-rootedness from our city lives during the summers between 1951 and 1955, felt as though we'd lost touch with the real world of city culture, upshot excitement and at least a great loss of individuality.

Campbell family Oroville Shanty 1954

After each summer when we returned to 402 Avalon Avenue, my life with friends and neighbors returned to normal. I'd reconnect with the spirits in the house, play with Bobby Harnwell in the empty lot and then within a couple of weeks the new school year would start.

As you can see from the Campbell kids' expressions in the next photograph, none of us liked summers at our Oroville shanty. The hot weather hindered wearing clothes or walking around. Just standing we'd sweat. Without a bathroom and running water, mom would have Timmy, Karen and I take morning walks down the road to the pub to fill up six-gallon jugs with water from their outside water spigot, with the owner's permission of course.

One time a wild turkey that roamed around the pub's property attacked me, jumping on my back, clawing my skin and pecking my head. Timmy came to the rescue and pulled the frigging feathered giant off me. Attacked, clawed and pecked by a turkey was science fiction to me.

We'd then have to walk a hundred yards back home up a slight grade, carrying the heavy water jugs, sweating all the way. I'd always wondered why me as the youngest child I had to participate in that chore, but I didn't ask. I was the smallest and weakest kid and had to pull my share of the work.

Left front: Joyce, Benny, Timmy
Left back: Karen, Ronnie
Not so happy Campbell kids in Oroville

The incendiary effects of the Oroville ecosystem at the hottest time of the day, around three in the afternoon, had me playing and bathing in the small creek beside our shanty. I'd lie in the shallow water in my bathing suit and splash the refreshing liquid over my body. When the water was drying out I'd damn up the creek with dirt, sticks and rocks and pray for rain.

My first prayer in Oroville would come true when we'd return to San Francisco during late August heat to prepare for the new school year. My second prayer was to not return to Oroville for another summer, ever. The shanty was dirty and creepy and filled with spiders. The crazy notion that mom spoke about, was that the scorching, stuffy weather helped relieve her arthritic pain. My young uninformed brain didn't understand her crazy notion.

As well-mannered kids, we attended public schools and were respectful of others if they didn't give us the creeps, so why wouldn't the Campbell kids be expecting something momentous and distinguished to come our way? I mean, we jockeyed for positions, and for all intents and purposes, as a new nuclear family, a financially viable social unit with complexities of horrific family disputes, dreadful arguments, appalling decisions and gruesome confrontations with shocking endings equaled a new breed.

Living at 402 Avalon Avenue was like monkey see, monkey do, acting like there's no tomorrow, kicking up our heels and knocking down mountains, and last but not least, all of us were counting our chickens before they were hatched. But not me, I was the observer, the youngest child who didn't want to make mistakes my older siblings had made. I watched, listened and learned and kept my mouth shut. Sometimes I'd shut my mouth so tight my lips hurt until mom would tell me that everything was okay. Then I'd go into the garage and dig more coins out of the dirt and feel someone was watching over me. How clever was that, feeling happy and digging in dirt healed all my adolescent fears?

The big city life of San Francisco during the 1950s was filled with infinite cultural, social, racial, political, ethnic and sexual evolution movements. They were clear manifestations of behavioral transformations, ethnic insurgencies and the arts that imitated radical upheavals in every aspect of city life. To me, those circumstances modernized all things American.

This is my story. Some events were golden conflicts and others were million-dollar episodes worth their weight in shaping my personality beginning in the confines of our musty, mildew, dry-rotted, and what some people had believed was a spooky house.

Throughout this work I've taken the liberty to alter literary rules by not using quotation marks denoting dialog. Instead, I've combined dialog with storytelling, which creates a smooth continuous flow to the narrative. Once again, throughout the pages are photos as complimentary visuals, pictures taken by family members.

Benny & Family

HERE ARE a few facts. I was born in Allegheny General Hospital, 320 E. North Avenue, Pittsburgh, Pennsylvania, on Wednesday January 17, 1945 at 4:04 PM. As an average baby weighing seven pounds four ounces why was I chubby. Possessing the usual arms and legs, eyes, ears and button-nose, all accentuated with a round, bald head, I was the sixth and last child of my parents. They named me Albert Benjamin Campbell; Albert was my dad's name and Benjamin was my mom's father name. Mom wanted my first name to be Benjamin but dad wouldn't settle for that, he wanted me to be named after him. Albert is my first name on my birth certificate, but mom always called me Benny. She loved styling my hair to resemble Clarabell the Clown. So, what did that make me?

Albert Benjamin Campbell 1946

Here is some hearsay as told to me by my mom, MinAleta Campbell; my dad's job at Bethlehem Steel transferred him from Pittsburgh to San Francisco in March 1945. My parents gathered and packed up all their furniture and clothing, including their five children. Mom gave birth to six children, but her third child, Patricia, had passed away at a young age from spinal meningitis. I was the youngest at two months.

They stuffed us in a Ford and started their long trek across the country to San Francisco where a job awaited my dad in the Navy Ship Yards at Bethlehem Shipbuilding Corporation. Two thirds of the way to California their trailer blew a tire. They didn't have a spare tire so they left the trailer on the side of the road. That was like The Grapes of Wrath all over again.

Having to start life over as husband and wife with five children ages two months to ten years of age in an unknown California environment was, at best, cathartic yet thrilling.

The Unites States was in the throes of World War II (WWII) that would end later that year on August 14, 1945. My mother, MinAleta (Larimore was her maiden name) Campbell, born April 23, 1915, was beginning to suffer the crippling effects of rheumatoid arthritis at 29 years of age. My father was bogged down having to drag his large family three thousand miles across country at 30 years of age.

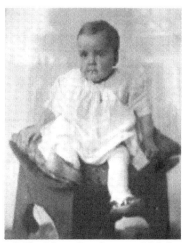

MinAleta Larimore 1916

Mom had left her entire family in Butler, Pennsylvania. Her father was Benjamin Larimore and her step-mother was Marie. Her mother Jessie Larimore (McKarns was her maiden name) had died when my mom was 14 years old. My mother's one sister Emma, who was about five years older, had passed away from sugar diabetes. They were all born and raised in

Butler, Pennsylvania.

Albert Edwin Campbell 1915

My father, Albert Edwin Campbell, born November 9, 1914, from which I'd been told by mom, was raised in Eau Claire, Pennsylvania, where he was an only child. They lived in a house-tent. They raised pigs, some cattle and sheep. My dad's Aunt Rose and Uncle Albert Smith were brother and sister. Neither had married and neither had children. They owned a pig and corn farm in Eau Claire and grew their own food. I was told that they built the two-story, four-bedroom house and lived in their special dwelling until they passed away sometime in the 1970s.

    I'd met Rose and Albert on two occasions, once during the summer of 1956 when Mom, Tim, Karen and I drove across the country to Pennsylvania and stayed for a week at granddaddy Ben's house in Butler. On that trip we'd visited Rose and Albert a couple of times in Eau Claire. My second encounter with Rose and Albert was during the summer of 1962 after I'd graduated from Sequoia High School in Redwood City, California. Mom, Ronnie and I drove back east and we stayed at Rose and Albert home for one week. I helped Albert hunt to kill any possums and raccoons that would eat his corn plants, but we didn't find any. I'd also helped Rose prepare dinners of freshly picked corn and green beans while she prepared meatloaf.

    From what I know Rose and Albert were dad's only relatives. Their lives were meek yet difficult. Their middle-aged bodies were weathered and deteriorating. What I loved most about them was their modest sense of humor and old-fashioned ethics. They said prayers before each meal, didn't swear, always washed their hands and when they had to sneeze or cough they'd excuse themselves and leave the room. They were in their mid-seventies when we'd visited them during 1962. They loved mom and were pleased to see me after six years.

While mom was growing up in Butler, her father worked at the local utility company. My mother's mom was a stay-at-home mom, and then later her step-mom was a stay-at-home mom helping to raise Carl, my mom's younger brother. I wish I had more information about the lives and times of Benjamin and Jessie Larimore and mom's brothers Howard and Carl, but I don't. As for mom's step-mother Marie, I know nothing about her life before marrying my granddad.

On our first trip back east in 1956 I'd met three cousins; one son and twin daughters of Howard Larimore. About the same age of eleven to fifteen we felt compatible. That was the last time I'd seen or talked to them or heard anything about them.

Two years ago, I'd met a man over the Internet who was the husband of a great-great granddaughter of Benjamin Larimore's sister. He emailed a photo of my supposed great-great grandmother Ellen Rebecca Stillwagon Sowash, whom he said was Benjamin Larimore's mother. However, the man was at that time attempting to locate documents as proof that Sowash was Benjamin's mother, but he didn't respond to my newer emails requesting more information.

My intention is not to make my story a family tree symposium. I suppose if I'd spent about ten thousand dollars for extensive family research, a family tree if you will, perhaps I'd have discovered facts and photos and relatives I'd thought didn't exist. None of that interested me. I've always been one to look forward and not look back. If the past had determined my future, then so be it. I thought that a little background information about the Campbell and Larimore relatives would be helpful understanding what the San Francisco Campbell family was about.

Ellen Rebecca Stillwagon Sowash
Benjamin Larimore's mother

How my parents met is sketchy. Mom told me they'd met at a dance, some type of social gathering. However, I was skeptical about that because my dad wasn't a social type as was mom. He possibly waited outside the dancehall over a period of weeks during dances then stalked mom afterwards until she said, "I do" to marriage. He was a handsome Sean Connery type in those days, nineteen years old, shy and determined. Mom was a Claudette Colbert type beauty, eighteen years of age, always smiling, never assuming, always accommodating and never complaining. They were a pleasant looking young couple and had a whole life ahead of them.

As a young married couple (I don't know their date of marriage) they had lived in Oakmont, a borough in Allegheny County and a Pittsburgh suburb in Pennsylvania. Life was difficult during freezing winters and blistering hot summers, trying to feed and raise five children. I have a few photos of Ronnie, Joyce and Timmy during a couple of winters, dressed in layered clothing and posing for the photos outside in the snow covered, muddy ground.

I was born a little over ten years after mom and dad were married. Was mom's last pregnancy a mistake? I never pondered the idea or heard a comment from my parents that I was a planned birth. I was their sixth child in the brood. During her pregnancy with me she had the beginning effects of rheumatoid arthritis, and two years after my birth she was using crutches to help her walk.

As a youngster I was fearful that her arthritis was transferred to me while I was in her womb. She reassured me that the condition wasn't transferrable and not to worry.

MinAleta Campbell   Al Campbell

The Projects at Hunter's Point, San Francisco is where my parents settled when I was two months old. I retain snippets of memories living in an apartment in the Projects, riding my tricycle around with Karen or Timmy when I was about four years old. San Francisco's Bay loomed down the distant hillside and I recall seeing huge ships drifting by.

Joyce is standing in back.
Front row left to right: Timmy, Karen and Ronnie.
March 1943 Oakmont, PA

At the Bethlehem Steel Corporation Shipbuilding Division in San Francisco my dad helped build submarines that would submerge into the Pacific and bear down on Japan. After WWII had ended my dad went to work for Southern Pacific Railroad, and that was when he started earning money.

Sometime around 1948 as a temporary residence until we moved into our huge wooden farmhouse at 402 Avalon, we had moved out of the Projects and into a house on Gerard Street across Bayshore Boulevard near Silver Avenue. The neighborhood was residential and windy and cold and from what I remember our home was comfortable.

Benny 1948 Hunter's Point, San Francisco, CA

Recalling something, just one tiny memory while living at the Gerard home was when my mom snapped a photo of me sitting on the floor beside our dog Missy. She was half-and-half Spitz and collie, white semi-long fur, black ears, a black diamond on her forehead and one large black blotch on her left side. Missy and I shared the same age. Mom and dad had adopted her as a puppy.

Nothing central comes to mind about our home on Gerard Street, just that the house was a stock San Francisco cutout squeezed between other houses on a semi-busy street and, it was a transition to important future critical family struggles; puzzling obstacles between dad and Ronnie and Joyce; an evil disease inside my mother; challenges for Timmy; struggles for Karen and lonely obstacles for me to overcome.

If I had recollections of moving from Gerard Street to 402 Avalon Avenue they're now forgotten. Being about five years old and starting kindergarten, with too much to learn and not enough educational space in my damn brain to remember little or big details I would fail. I do recall that neither my parents nor my siblings offered me preschooler emotional support, as I now believe was the case for my siblings when they were my age.

Timmy & Karen 1948 Hunter's Point

Across Madrid Street from our new home on Avalon Avenue was a slanted two-acre empty lot full of healthy tall milkweeds and sticky-wet crabgrass. I had tons of fun sliding down the steep hillside covered with dry grass during the summers, and even more fun digging a few deep tunnels that would extend ten to fifteen feet. Inside the tunnels I'd play with my dump truck and a few plastic toy army soldiers. On the far end of the empty lot down the block was the quaint yet cathartic Monroe Elementary School, my new school where I was rushed to get to school on time and at the speed of light the school would house me for the next six years.

Not to my surprise that was where I'd be persuaded to accept socializing, where I'd be inundated and christened with a fundamental education, where I'd sing in the glee-club to my excitement, work the streets as a panicky crossing guard after school, win almost every game playing marbles on the asphalt playground, targeting to kick a large rubber ball over the six foot tall cyclone wire fence while playing kickball, slam the tetherball into my opponents head, and parade around the playground for the silly May Day Celebrations.

Timmy, Benny, Karen in front row
Joyce, Ronnie in back row
Gerard Street, San Francisco, CA

    To my recollection the May Day Celebrations were not mindless, they were pointless. Teachers would decorate the flagpole, assign the girls with boy dancing partners then at lunchtime, make us prance around the poll by wrapping narrow rolls of different colored crepe paper around it. To me the celebration was pointless, but to the teachers the festivities were beneficial, traditional, and thus ringing in springtime. Prancing in a circle made me dizzy but the carnival celebrations got us out of practicing penmanship.
    Recess times were energizing and my superlative social times in school. I'd win small paper bags full of marbles, exchange peanut butter sandwiches for Twinkies, and become an expert kickball kicker and a tetherball aficionado.

ON WEEKENDS with my neighbor Bobby Harnwell, like ninjas we'd climb the six-foot tall chain-link fence a dozen times that surrounded the entire Monroe Elementary School yard. On many Saturdays I'd roller skate crisscrossing the playground asphalt a hundred times with my unbalanced sister Karen. She wasn't proficient at stopping or turning while skating. One time she'd sped across the yard and unable to turn away fast enough she smashed both shins against the wooded bench beside the brick wall. She fell, took off her skates and threw them across the school yard. Over the next two weeks she limped and her shin bruises turned purple and yellow. That was the funniest thing I'd ever seen.

Benny & Roller Skates 1954

For the ensuing six years after moving into the dilapidated three-story, square farmhouse, I'd cross the street at the intersection of Avalon Avenue and Madrid Street and walk the sidewalk to Monroe School three hundred feet down the block every school day just before 8:00 a.m. Ready or not, I'd enter the two-story red-brick school building, the dry smell of chalk and the feeling of dampness followed me as I'd walk two long hallways and entered my classroom.

While sitting behind my appointed desk that had a round hole at the top for an ink well, I'd bite my lips, skid my fingertips across the desktop and test my academic brain to learn how to read, write letters in cursive and add and subtract. What good was any of that? At least three school days a week at lunchtime I'd walk home to mom's cooked meals such as scrambled eggs and fried potatoes, or an egg salad sandwich, or reheated meatloaf, or a bacon, lettuce and tomato sandwich and even a piece of heated apple pie with vanilla cream.

After school around 3:10 p.m., I'd return home to build a better me by learning the lessons of life by watching *Howdy Doody,* and Captain Kangaroo, or the puppet show *Time for Beany* on television.

My environment of applied, practical self-preservation in the Campbell family consisted of Mom and dad and my siblings each leaving on personal errands. Every day after school I fell into my own little world until dinner time. Mom had me help her cook, wash the dishes and then afterwards, I'd retire to what I needed to get done. Did I have homework to do? Yes, all the time, but history, math and English had to wait until Karen and I were finished playing the *Go Fish* card game. After homework I was allowed to watch two half-hours or one-hour television shows with the family.

Monroe Elementary School 1956

We watched sitcoms like *The Honeymooners* with Jackie Gleason and *The Life of Riley* starring William Bendix, and other nights we'd watch the crime drama *Highway Patrol* starring Broderick Crawford, or *The Bob Cummings Show* starring Robert Cummings, or we watched *I Love Lucy* with Lucille Ball. We watched so many shows from the 1950s era that I'd have to Google to recall more of their titles. If you have Netflix or streaming videos from amazon.com or iTunes, you might get a few laughs form those 1950s TV shows.

Foggy mornings didn't dissuade me from walking to school for those six years. No matter how scary the weather was, the dense fog from May to June would veil the empty lot and obscure Monroe Elementary School from sight. Walking in the fog was refreshing when the air itself seemed alive with possibilities.

Dashing my small alarmed-self to school, and at least absorbing some education by-the-book, if not all the material my instructors wanted me to learn, I was evolving into an adolescent encyclopedia of American history; memorizing the dates of the American Revolution, the Civil War, U.S. involvement in WWII and the Korean War, locating cities and states on a map of the U.S., as well as memorizing all the U.S. Presidents beginning with the current Dwight D. Eisenhower and backwards, and becoming an authority on the constitution of the United States, the amendments and the three branches of government.

One specific day while sitting at my classroom desk, my teacher Mrs. Hunt directed the students to write a complete sentence describing our houses.

I wrote a complete sentence about democratic equality in the family instead of writing about my house, which didn't set well with Mrs. Hunt. She'd gathered up all the papers from the children and read their sentences in front of the class until she came to mine. Her eyes drifted across the page. She looked at me, skipped reading my effort and placed the paper on her desk. I was shocked. Equality in the classroom was missing. My favorite teacher Mrs. Hunt hated me now.

After school she dismissed my classmates and called me to her desk. I stood in front of her desk ready to be reprimanded.

She looked at me, her lips parted, ready to squawk.

When I assign the class a task such as writing a complete sentence that describes your house, I expect you to do the same, Mrs. Hunt said. Can you do that for me and not write about anything else instead?

Yes, mam. I lowered my eyes, feeling rejected, knowing that I'd failed the assignment.

Mrs. Hunt spoke again. This time, Benny, your sentence about equal opportunity between family members is original. I'll pass you on this assignment, but you have to remember to follow my instructions.

I raised my eyes. Yes, mam.

You can go now. She said. But I want you to remember to always be original and express your opinion, just not with one of my assignments.

Yes, mam.

After leaving school that day I went home and asked mom if I could sweep the floors in the house and take the garbage out. She was pleased and handed me the broom.

Monroe Elementary School intersection of Madrid Street and Excelsior Avenue where I was a crossing guard.

Untangling the English language and unraveling mathematical equations frustrated my *keep it simple* mind. Confrontations with learning while trying to grasp the perplexities of geology and geography baffled my mind's eye. The real brainteaser for me was attempting to understand the mysteries of human behavior. Just why kids cried and screamed because they didn't want to read in front of the class, or spit on and kick each other during recess because they didn't want to sit in specific chairs, and why our teachers would jump down many student's throats, grab them by their arms and drag them out of the classroom and into the hallway, seemed overkill to me. A few of us buckled under the strain and became introverted, the rest were aligned students, absorbing everything they could for fear of getting their hands slapped with a ruler.

Social behavior unnerved me. Understanding indulgent social sport activities like car racing where accidents happen and drivers got killed, when two men boxed the brains out of each other, when rodeos were held and injuries to animals and people happened, and the biggest event of all for me, I struggled to understand the social sport of war when countries invaded each other, bombed and maimed and killed just for dominance and power.

At first my teachers laughed at my questions about those subjects. When I persisted, they were displeased and bothered like dark-lord converts. While my classmates giggled about my questions I'd become my teachers' worst enemy in 3rd-5th grades, except for Mrs. Hunt in the 6th grade, and they would ignore me or send me to the Principal's office. The Principal told me a few times throughout the years that I was to follow my teacher's instructions and not ask distracting or trivial question that didn't relate to school work. Little did he know?

Interspersed within those six years, we had at least six weeks during each summer living at our shanty in Oroville. After school let out in June for the summer, the Campbell kids had two weeks to get into trouble before they left for Oroville. When we came home to San Francisco two or three weeks before the next school year started in September, we had time left to cause anxiety to our parents or distress the neighborhood kids and their parents, and one other thing, we'd played outside too late in the evening.

As a child, like any other child, I'd looked at things without judging and without prejudice. I'd tried to understand events on fundamental and practical levels because that was all I knew, thus I heard, watched and learned from social interactions and academic instructions, and understood that life began for me when my memory kicked in at about six years of age in the first grade. During that time in 1951 all hell broke loose at 402 Avalon.

I needed to learn the truth about my family and the reasons why a layered silence, equaling a silent prayer, held us together. I wanted to know why mom and dad argued behind their closed bedroom door, why Ronnie was mean to me and Joyce was aloof, and why Timmy and Karen had all the freedom they wanted, but I didn't. I was not *The Boy Who Cried Wolf*, although my siblings said that I was.

San Francisco

SAN FRANCISCO was a city of way too many amazing features; fantastic landscapes, proprietary character, and highlights that had to be experienced. I wanted the hills to be steeper, the parks bigger, the buildings taller, the bridges wider, and the freeways were beginning to be constructed.

Elmer Edwin Robinson (October 3, 1894 – June 9, 1982) was the 33rd mayor of San Francisco, California. As a Republican, he served as San Francisco's mayor from January 1948 until January 1956. He promoted and oversaw numerous development projects, including an expansion of San Francisco International Airport and the construction of new schools, libraries, police stations, parking garages, and the modernization of the San Francisco Municipal Railway.

During the 1950s freeways were designed for inside and around San Francisco, which would open up the City for quick transit. But for us kids, local buses, electric and trolley cars offered transfers that were good for an entire day. I could ride the bus all over the City for ten cents and not get lost.

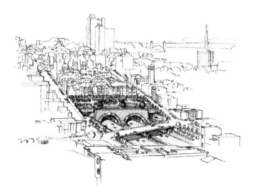

This was a plan for an 8-lane freeway to cut under Russian Hill on the way from the Embarcadero to the Golden Gate Bridge.

The California Division of Highways had a plan to extend freeways across San Francisco. At that time the freeway reigned supreme in California, but San Francisco citizens harbored the seeds of an emerging revolt which saved several neighborhoods from the wrecking ball and also started the first serious opposition to the post-WW II consensus about restricting automobile parking, the construction of freeways, and suburbanization of San Francisco.

The San Francisco Chronicle published a map of the proposed and actual freeway routes through San Francisco even though the editorial had already chased away protestors that were against them.

George Christopher was elected mayor of San Francisco in November 1955 and took office the following January. He was instrumental in bringing the New York Giants baseball team to San Francisco in 1958 (where they became the San Francisco Giants) and in securing funding to build Candlestick Park on the abandoned lands of Sunset Scavenger on Candlestick Point. The ballpark opened for the Giants 1960 season. Christopher's administration is credited with the building of Brooks Hall, twelve new schools, seventeen firehouses, six public swimming pools, the five-story Fifth and Mission and the underground Civic Center garages.

Distant Downtown San Francisco 1950

That was my San Francisco during the 1950s. No matter how much I try to undress the City, San Francisco always had a pristine soul. If there ever was a replica of a city San Francisco was that reproduction. The City was an exciting playground built yesterday for business gold-diggers as well as to impress tourists.

To me the City was a gigantic movie set that resembled eye-catching cities in the movies. Yet, was the City a fantasy, a metropolis that was even on planet earth? Yes, and best of all San Francisco was in the liberal state of California. What better city and state to be raised in? The metropolis was socially fashionable and culturally important, a leader in many paths to future developments that were endemic and emblematic to San Francisco's communal alterations.

Eight months after George Christopher took office, and after our long two-month road-trip across the States to New York and back during the summer of 1956, my mother MinAleta decided she wanted to move to Tucson, Arizona. We'd holed up for a few days in Tucson on our way home from visiting our relatives in Pennsylvania. Even before Tucson, mom had decided that dry desert weather would work wonders against her rheumatoid arthritis as opposed to the ideally cool, moist climate of San Francisco. She'd given the Pacific Ocean weathered City a try for eleven years while her health deteriorated. With her doctor's acknowledgement she decided that the desert weather would suit her physical condition better. Later on, for your entertainment, I'll explain more about our move to Tucson, Arizona.

John McLaren Park

The benefits of living in San Francisco were many during the 1950s. The Wanderlust City consisted of man-made muses

and had countless natural vistas to witness. If I had enough material to blanket the city, I'd have enveloped and zipped closed city life for posterity.

The *49-Mile Scenic Drive* sign was designed by a local artist named Rex May. His design won the 1955 competition held by San Francisco's Downtown Association. Along the drive you'll see City Hall, Coit Tower, Golden Gate Bridge, Palace of Fine Arts, the Bay Bridge, Lombard Street and many more panoramas and landscapes.

I was fortunate enough to see most everything in the City by crisscrossing the neighborhoods via bus and Trolley Car transfers from Ghirardelli Square to the Ferry Building at the end of Market Street, to McLaren Park, to Ocean Beach and Playland, to the Golden Gate Bridge then the Bay Bridge and from there across town to the Cow Palace on Geneva Avenue, Daly City. I even climbed up Mt. Davidson to the cross one afternoon and was completely exhausted.

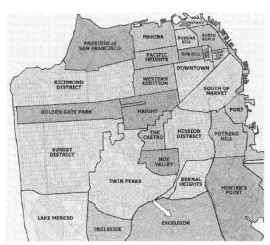

San Francisco Excelsior District

Mom loved driving in the City. Twin Peaks was a common destination as was Ocean Beach, Playland, the Cliff House, Golden Gate Park, Fleishhacker Zoo and Fleishhacker Pool; the world's largest heated salt-water pool. A couple of times she drove across the Golden Gate Bridge to visit Sausalito. On sunny weekend days she'd drive us to visit Ghirardelli Square for hot chocolate or ice cream then swim in the cold waters of

Aquatic Park across from the Square. Fisherman's wharf was a destination to get a touristy fix then on Sundays almost before sunrise we'd head over to the Farmer's Market on Alemany Boulevard and purchase fresh vegetables and fruits for the entire week. A couple Halloweens we'd cross the busy Alemany Boulevard to be in the nice Bernal Heights neighborhood for trick-or-treating.

Mayor George Christopher was instrumental with redevelopment projects of major portions of city and private lands that were labeled Slums in the late 1950s. Japan Town and the Fillmore urban renewal displaced African-Americans and the remnants of the Jewish Community for concrete high-rises, the new Hall of Justice and the opening of the Embarcadero Freeway, which blocked the Embarcadero and Ferry Building from the city, which spawned the first Freeway Revolt. But overall the City was now a wonderland of visuals.

San Francisco was mine to embrace as the City was for the other 775,357 residents in 1955, of which 693,888 were Caucasians.

Mt. Davidson Cross under lit

Our neighborhood was the Excelsior District and it was famous as a multi-cultural community. It's located along Mission Street, east of San Jose Ave, west of John McLaren Park and north of Geneva Avenue. Culturally mixed but not racially varied back in my day, our neighbors consisted of first and second European generations. A few of my elementary school classmates were first-generation Americans. Their parents dressed different and spoke English with their native language accents if they spoke English at all. The families were Russian, Italian, Greek, French, German and Portuguese.

A feature of the Excelsior District is that many streets are named after national capitals such as London, Lisbon, Madrid, Edinburgh, Naples, Vienna, Dublin, Athens, Moscow, Munich and Prague, or famous universities such as Cambridge, Oxford, Yale, Princeton and Amherst, as well as countries such as Brazil, Peru, Russia, France and Italy. I didn't know what any of those names meant until I was about ten years old and they were an indelible part of our colorful neighborhood.

Right in the center of the Excelsior district is Avalon Avenue and in the center of Avalon Avenue during those years was our house at 402 Avalon Avenue, our big wooden farm house that was about seventy years old, deteriorating and worst of all, without maintenance.

402 Avalon Avenue

THE CAMPBELL KIDS, Timmy, Karen and I were always ready for action. We didn't claim to be anything special yet we had distinct personalities that attracted neighborhood kids. We were three ordinary kids that lived in a huge one-of-a-kind house that was perhaps inhabited by disembodied ghouls, who may have been former residents that committed heinous crimes, or who were just familiar with the house, and that was the drawing card for us.

Since I'd realized that the ghouls inhabiting my home were friendly sprits, my belly-laughs were many and intense expression elevated kids' faces when I'd ask them to come to play at my house.

The neighborhood kids and my schoolmates were fearful, but many of them were intrigued and were destined to experience the haunted house.

To me, the tall rectangular structure of 402 Avalon was designed to create feelings of balance and unity but sitting atop a chunky dug-out garage into the hillside and surrounded by the tall funky fence gave the house an ominous city ambiance. The kids that came to our house were masked with anxiety, some were impressed others were hesitant, and when they came over we'd played in the area behind the eight-foot-high fence that enclosed our side yard and driveway, which led to the garage/basement dug into the hillside.

Our neighbor Bobby Elliot resembled the fictional character Eddie Haskell on the Leave It to Beaver television comedy. He was sneaky and he would come into dad's workshop with Tim to make wooden puppets with dad's tools. I'd caught him a couple of times trying to sneak through the door and climb the stairs to the second floor on his way to invade our attic.

Bobby Elliot was a smart kid, a little brash for me, you know, swaggering and smug like a pit bull. But I felt that his problems with his sister and mother attributed to his parading personality. He was a groupie to the Campbell Kids Gang and wanted our mom to adopt him.

My friend and neighbor Bobby Harnwell would come over and play with me in the driveway or garage. A few times he went with me into dad's workshop to ogle at tools and touch things. We'd watch dad work on his projects until he'd tell us to go play somewhere else. Bobby came inside our house many times but he preferred to stay outside in the driveway, where he could breathe fresh air and feel safe looking at his house across the street from us on Avalon Avenue.

My friend and school mate Richard Patoni said that his mother wouldn't allow him to go to our house. She'd believed the haunted stories that circulated, and that whatever disease crippled my mom, for the safety of her oldest son from becoming crippled, she forbade him to come over. Richard wasn't afraid of our house but he respected his mother's demand and never came to visit me. We'd talk over the telephone, meet at school and walk around the neighborhood, but he never came to play at 402 Avalon.

My friends James and Marjorie and Yvonne were classmate whom I jib-jabbed with every day at school, but I never did invite them over to my house. When I was older I'd felt embarrassed living at the old haunted house. I wanted to lead a normal life by living at one of the newer stucco houses like my friends lived in. Their houses had newer roofs on them and the stucco was so white and clean. They had large blue and white flowered hydrangea plants growing beside their front steps, and their one car garage doors had automatic door openers. All of that was organized and pleasing to me and I needed to live their lives instead of mine.

But then if I'd lived in a house that resembled my friends I wouldn't have been the unique kid in the neighborhood, the curious and inspired kid that I was, living in a house with creaky doors, windows that were painted shut, floors that were more than cracked they were soft underfoot, walls that seemed to sway, ceilings with fissures, my family's house that was filled with tenants on the second floor and that crazy attic bathroom outcrop atop the roof that was creepy looking and permanently sealed off. If I didn't live in this house full of unidentified history and disjointed construction, nothing in my life would have fused together like the ability to hobnob with spirits. I'd just be another ordinary kid in the neighborhood, afraid of but longing to get inside that haunted house at 402 Avalon and experience the oddity.

402 Avalon Avenue, San Francisco, California

This is the single photograph I have of our house, and I think that was because mom had the only Kodak Number 2 box camera in our family. She took few photos of the house. She loved taking photos and had her own dark room for developing her snapshots. Her photo developing room was always off-limits to us kids because of the picture developing chemicals. Most of the photos of the family included in this book, mom had snapped and developed. On occasions she'd let me watch her developing photos. I recall seeing the string close line she had hung across the room with new photos clipped to the string and drying, via the traditional wood clothespin with springs. I'd detailed the above picture with arrows and descriptions.

402 Avalon Avenue could have been the *Hell House,* a novel by American novelist Richard Matheson before he had published it in 1971. And the house could have been *The Amityville Horror*: A True Story, the book by Jay Anson, published in September 1977.

Our home wasn't a house where parapsychologists attributed haunting to spirits of the dead and the effect of violent or tragic events in the building's past such as murder, accidental death, or suicide. The big old house was a big old house as I knew it, without a history of violent or tragic events. The dwelling was ours to explore, maddening at times, but nonetheless not haunted, well, maybe not haunted.

At my young age the ghost I'd known was the cartoon character *Casper the Friendly Ghost*. I didn't put much thought into a house haunted by ghosts. I was interested in the physical aspects of living and not anything that might happen after life. When I'd hear noises and not see anything and couldn't get a fix on or place the noise, I'd wonder if ghosts were actual spirits sequestered inside the house, or that the house was just creaky from ground movements.

When I was in the fifth grade I became more inquisitive about our home, and since my family inhabited most of the first floor, I started exploring the basement/garage at ground level and then the second floor and the attic. So much to explore in the three-story house, I'd continued to probe and examine everything I could. During the next two years until we vacated the house and had moved to Tucson in September 1956, the places I couldn't explore were the occupied apartments on the second floor.

I was forbidden by mom and dad to climb the stairs to the second floor and the attic. Their restriction didn't stop me when curiosity urged me like a strike of lightening to climb the claustrophobic twenty steep, creaky stairwell steps. They were in the center of the house through a door on the west side.

The second floor consisted of a long hallway to the left and right. With four, one-bedroom apartments, two on each side of the hallway, the second floor was complete. Across from the stairwell door in the hallway was another door that led to a confined stairwell that had eight secret rungs to the attic, an attic that still confuses me to this day because of neglect.

The second-floor apartments were always rented so I couldn't enter them. One emigrated Italian man was a tenant in the apartment over our living room. On Saturday afternoons he played his big accordion and kept time by stomping one foot on his floor, which was our ceiling. Mom would get her small red-pearled Elettra accordion and stridently pump out tunes in our living room to drown out the crazy Italian concerto coming through the floor. At times when his music was too loud she'd give me a broom to trump our ceiling. He would stop playing for the day then on Sunday morning he'd start playing again with his foot stomping.

MinAleta's Elletra Accordion

    The accordion was mom's instrument. Music would flow out of her pores when she played the beautiful little thing. Wearing a blue crepe blouse, the straps of the small Elettra fit perfectly over mom's small shoulders. Sitting in her wheelchair she held the lightweight accordion above her black cotton pants.
    Fluid and synchronized, mom's crooked fingers, stooped shoulders, bony elbows, kinked knees and diseased body would disappear, and she'd become a sweet angel in heaven. Playing the accordion was a sign of hope where she was completely at ease with her painful body.
    Standing in the hallway, listening to mom play the beautiful slow song *Auld Lang Syne* then smoothly switch to playing the high tempo *Way Down Upon the Swanee River*, made me want to learn how to play the accordion. After I'd told her that I'd like to learn she handed me the Elettra. I strapped the alien looking thing around my shoulders and tried to push the bellows back and forth. My clumsy fingers on both hands

wouldn't coordinate pushing the buttons and keys, making me believe I'd never learn how to whip the bellows back and forth and play respectable music.

MinAleta on the upside dirt driveway 1956

You're not musical, mom said. You won't learn how to play the accordion.
Can I learn to play the guitar?
You should go play with your dump truck.
I handed the accordion back to her.
Can I watch you play your accordion?
While mom played the song *How Much Is That Doggie in the Window* on her accordion, I got lost in the rhythm, went to the living room window and looked at the huge concrete cross on top of Mt. Davidson. Even though the cross was about 4 miles away across the valley I wanted it to be in the empty lot

across the street. That way I'd be closer to Jesus and maybe my prayers would be answered that mom's rheumatoid arthritis would disappear.

Was I being childish? Never! Would mom's rheumatoid arthritis vanish? Never!

A few minutes later I grabbed my dump truck off the floor in my bedroom and ran through the house to the backyard.

402 Avalon Avenue Backyard 1955

Around the back of the house was an outside stairwell that led to the second floor. The railing and stairs were unstable and I'd decided never to climb them, but I could drive my toy dump truck up and down the lower railing.

The large fenced backyard housed a four-line clothesline. The lines were ten feet long and their ends were attached to five-foot-tall metal rounded T-bars. I'd spent many hours during the year clipping up wet clothes to dry on the clothesline, and then spent a few hours taking down the dry clothes, folding them and putting them in a basket.

Our garden of various vegetables was squeezed for space because one-sixth of the backyard contained Ronnie's racing pigeon coups. The ground was dirt and stones so I didn't play out there very much. I played in the double wide large driveway on the upside of the house in front of the carriage house that was dad's workshop. Perhaps six, maybe eight cars could park on that dirt driveway. Dad spent uncountable hours underneath the hoods of cars, making mechanical repairs.

The 4-foot wide walkway deck on the front and side of the house was decorated with a 3-foot tall railing that wobbled in places. The unstable railing was supposedly secured with posts every eight feet. The exterior railing atop the outer fence served no purpose. The railing on the walkway deck was an avant-garde quantity of two-by-fours. But what the hell, I could fall under the railing and smash my big head on the hardened dirt eight feet below, but I knew better as well as did Missy, our happy, healthy dog.

I was injured once when I was seven years old in the lousy front yard that wasn't a yard. The area was a slanted driveway but used as a dump for discarded teardown wood framing from around the house. I was playing there with Missy, throwing a ball and I stepped on a rusty nail that was left sticking out of a rotted piece of wood. I screamed and dad came running out of his workshop, carried me inside to the kitchen, sat me down and pulled the nail out of my foot. Small droplets of blood dripped to the floor. Dad slipped my shoe and dirty sock off my foot. He stepped to the refrigerator and pulled something from a shelf and said, sit for fifteen minutes and hold this piece of hamburger on the nail hole. Hamburger will draw the poisons out.

Twenty minutes later mom washed and bandaged my foot.

Now go outside and play, she said.

A few weeks later Timmy had a five-pound marine line weight that was tied to a piece of long rope. He whipped the marine weight in a circle like a lasso, holding onto the other end of the rope. The weight flew over the stiff-wired clothesline, swung around and walloped Timmy in the forehead. My older brother's feet flipped up when he pummeled to the ground on his back. With the thump of his body dust spewed everywhere.

Self-inflicted concussions had to be a family trait.

A few weeks after that Karen fell off the roof of Monroe Elementary School onto the empty lot and broke an arm. Was that her right or left arm? I just remember the white cast, how dirty if got after a few weeks, how itchy her arm became and the funny smell of plaster and sweat by the time the doctor cut the cast off a couple of months later. Karen wasn't the most coordinated sister, but she was determined and tough.

There had to have been numerous injuries that took place in and around the house over the decades. Mr. Marshall dying from a heart attack in his studio apartment in the backside of the house was one fatality that happened while we lived there. His fat Jimmy Durante nose was one topic of accusations over the years between Timmy, Karen and me. When one of us would get angry with another we'd accuse each other of having a Mr. Marshall nose.

Overall, 402 Avalon Avenue was a secure, large and looming entity, sometimes dreaded because of being a fire-hazard and sometimes a few neighbors worried about the unusual Campbell family and occupants.

Dad's business partner, Mr. Cooper resembled Edward G. Robinson. He was the cigar yielding, hat wearing actor and is best remembered for his roles as gangsters, such as Rico in his star-making film Little Caesar and as Rocco in Key Largo.

Mr. Cooper and my dad worked on inventing products such as the Cal-Cor, a tiny hand-held fire extinguisher that would extinguish small fires without chemicals and the container was recyclable. The presence of Mr. Cooper around the house was limited to their projects and demonstrations of them to corporate byers.

Hey kid, Mr. Cooper would say to me, then pull on his cigar and pat me on the shoulders.

Dad's part-time life was detailed in the Carriage House at the upper-back side of 402 Avalon. The area was originally used to house horse carriages and farming equipment. In the nooks and crannies and including the upraised bedroom that was always locked, I'd say the area measured at least eight hundred square feet. The workshop was where we'd find dad when he was home.

He'd converted the entire area into a workshop, his paradise away from his family that housed all of his construction tools and equipment. The modern tools fascinated me and most were off-limits. The free-standing drill press and the large bench-saw always drew my attention. If you want to cut off a hand, dad said, or your arm or leg go ahead and play with the electric saw. See here, this is the on-off switch.

I ran from the workshop picturing my arms and legs on the sawdust floor, chopped off my body by the bench saw. Dad's laugh in the background echoed in my head.

Always drawn to the workshop when nobody was there, I'd inspect every inch of the room and made certain that I didn't touch the on-off switch on the bench saw. That damn bench saw wasn't going to chop off my hand, arm or leg.

Throughout the large shop I'd maneuver around the power tools, a couple of generators and different pieces of equipment to the backside, where a ten-foot-long workbench was positioned under windows that extended across the entire length of the room. The windows overlooked the garden and a sidebar of Ronnie's pigeon coups in the backyard. On top of the dusty, dirty bench were a series of at least ten discarded Maxwell House and Yuban one-pound size coffee cans as well as a dozen glass jam jars. They were lined up against the back wall, all of which housed an assortment of used nails, screws, washers and small pieces of aluminum, copper, brass and junk. Beside the right side of the bench was a door that led to the backyard.

At both ends of the workbench were two, three-foot-wide hallways, one to the left and one to the right. Each hallway housed compact compartments against the inner wall, and from the floor up to about three feet tall. The compartments were filled with all sizes and types of wood and all brightened by the light coming from the windows.

Back in the large workshop, the ceiling had rafters where two-by-fours were stored. Around the sides of the workshop, tools and more boards and sticks and bars of steel and brass and copper leaned against the walls. This shop was a workman's dream come true and dad, I know longed to be there working on projects or locked in his extra bedroom where we wouldn't bother him.

My fascination with dad's workshop was always too much for me. My eyes would hurt do to light streaming through the back windows, and with sunlight spears stabbing at dust particles in the air. When nighttime came I'd pull on the overhead string in the middle of the room and an illegal ceiling light would swing on its chain, shadowing the area.

Unusual noises would stop my curiosity whenever I was alone in the shop. My eyes would search for movement and—I knew spirits were present. Various odors of sawdust, oil, paint and sweat sometimes had me reeling to spring from the area. I'd close my eyes, working my mind overtime listening to distant noises of footsteps, glass breaking and just plain old creaking boards. When I'd open my eyes, I'd be drifting out of the workshop and into the house.

I'd jump down one step into the vestibule that had a door that opened onto the upside driveway. Ignoring that door, I'd run across the short room, jump up one step and enter the hallway that led to a tiny half-bath and two small bedrooms where Ronnie, Timmy and I slept. I'd run into our large kitchen where I'd be silent in case family members were around because I was happiest when alone.

Throughout the years from six years old in 1951 and on, I felt lonesome like a snail and indifferent inside. With no direction and without guidance, I was an abandoned child, so on times when I was alone I'd go to the living room on the other side of the house, turn on our Admiral TV council and watch nonsense news being televised about a war in Korea and a man named Truman that directed a uniformed man named MacArthur. Another channel showed a bald man named Eisenhower and his funny looking teammate named Nixon, waving and signing papers and looking official like they were posing for painters to brush their portraits.

Activity was happening inside my home. When I wasn't looking inward I'd be listening to conversations between mom and dad. Sometimes they had heated arguments and other times their voices were soft with laughter. Feisty cussing arguments between them were about Ronnie and Joyce; quarrels about Ronnie learning a working profession instead of attending San Francisco City college, and squabbles about how Joyce dressed, had a tomboy haircut and about her younger boyfriend.

One topic of discussion between them centered around 402 Avalon. I didn't get many facts but I'd overheard them talking about various upgrades throughout the decades and that the house still wasn't safe to live in, that someday the house or property would be valuable. If they were talking about selling the house, I didn't know. Whoever would want to purchase the spirit besieged 402 Avalon would be as mad as a hatter.

Other than listening to mom and dad's arguing voices behind the walls and watching television news shows and other shows like the *Howdy Doody* show with Buffalo Bob Smith, the *Amos and Andy* sitcom, *I love Lucy*, *Kukla Fran and Ollie*, *The Phil Silvers Show* and a few others if time allowed, I'd go outside on the upside driveway and play with my toy, plastic soldiers. Other times I'd go under the house into the garage with one of dad's old screwdrivers and dig in the hard dirt on the side of a berm, searching for that one treasure that would change my life, coins.

At six years old I didn't know much, but I knew about time. I was learning how to read time in the first grade but didn't own a wristwatch. I knew that time twisted and turned and sped forward and history was filled with it, yet time was limited and never in my favor.

When I was making headway understanding how life worked in the Campbell family at 402 Avalon, mom would yell at me when I was playing in the dirt driveway, telling that lunch or dinner was ready, or Joyce would yell out that bedtime was now, or Ronnie would yell to reprimand me for something mindless like needing the screwdriver I was using. Dad had twenty other screwdrivers in his workshop. Other times Ronnie told me that I was irresponsible and stupid for being so young, or that I'd never be as smart as he was. He'd punch my shoulder. I'd hold steady on my feet.

You should come and take Judo lessons with me, Ronnie said.

What the heck was Judo and why did he punch me? The next day a bruise appeared on my shoulder.

Time was my enemy because I knew that 402 Avalon was going to swallow me and I'd never return for lunch or dinner, or go to bed, or become responsible and smart for being so young, and never reach for the sky and become more intelligent than Ronnie. After uncountable times over the years having thoughts like those I'd just pinch my left shoulder and say: I'm six years old, or seven, or eight or nine years old and tell myself that I was just a kid lost in a big world of stupidity.

Mom saw the bruise on my shoulder. Did you fall down and hurt yourself?

Ronnie slugged me and said I should take Judo lessons with him.

Maybe you should, Benny. You might gain some confidence learning Judo.

I'M GOING to take you inside the three-story splinter of wood and show in detail what 402 Avalon looked and felt like, at least what I can recall. Over fifty-seven years have passed since I'd lived there but overall the house is unforgettable.

Dad had ongoing building projects on the first floor in the backside of the house in the large vacant room behind our living quarters and next to his workshop. He partitioned the area into what I believed to be a studio apartment with a nicely appointed bathroom with a shower.

From my memory twenty rooms in the entire house was enough, and I think maybe two more were added in the apartment dad had built. Dad was changing much of the first-floor interior of the house between 1950 and 1956 that I didn't pay much attention to. I played on top of the discarded pieces of wood or collected bent nails off the floor and with my slingshot would shoot them into our backyard or across the street into the empty lot.

The photo of 402 Avalon was taken from across the street at the top corner of the large vacant lot. Behind that eight-foot-tall fence that ran along the entire property down Madrid Street, two extra-wide doors opened inward to a gaping dirt driveway. The entire rectangular area inside the fence was about fifteen feet deep by about forty feet long and was exposed to all weather elements.

Inside the fence to the left side of the garage driveway was a large bank of dirt that was always covered with crabgrass, broken bottles and discarded tin cans. Sometimes I played on top of the mound but I was afraid of incurring injury from all the broken glass. To the right side of the driveway was a flat hardened area which was part of the dirt driveway. A car could park there kitty-corner. Under the house two more extra-wide doors opened that revealed a large excavated parking area that could house about four cars. Tall posts were strategically placed on concrete blocks that rose up and supported the flooring joist beams overhead.

At the backside of the dugout garage was a mound of hardened dirt about two feet high with jagged edges. That was my treasure chest. I'd discovered hundreds of coins buried in the dirt and when I needed money I'd sneak into the garage and dig up dimes and quarters, wash them at a water spigot outside and store them inside a small Tabaco bag I took from dad's workshop.

Outside of the tall fence the door next to the garage door led to an outside stairwell that led up to walkway decking. That walkway was fifteen feet long from the fence to the first floor of the house. The doorway at the end of that walkway led to the second-floor stairwell. To the right of the stairwell door were two more doors on the side of the building that led to studio apartments. The walkway continued from there to the backside of the house where a gated fence led to the backyard. To the left of the stairwell door were two large windows and a walkway that ran along the side of our living room and around the corner to our front door. Our dog Missy would stand at the corner of the house waiting to greet anyone with a smile.

Along the bottom edge of the outside fence, dead weeds were always present in the two-foot-wide space of dirt between the sidewalk and fence. A gardener wasn't needed and I'd always wondered just why no one in my family ever mowed down the dead weeds since dad had built and sold electric lawnmowers. My family was negligent to ground maintenance and they just didn't think about curb-appeal or attractive neighborhood appearance.

The wooded fence was perfect for bouncing a tennis ball against or for targeting knife throwing. When I was older and bored, the fence was the target for my switchblade. Every boy who had two dollars to spend owned a switchblade. I'd purchased mine from the Ben Franklin store on Mission Street. I'd educated myself on the uses of a knife and was careful not to stick myself or cut off a finger when I'd spring the switchblade open and close. Mine had a safety button that prevented it from opening in my pants pocket and hand. I'd stand about six feet away from the fence and with an overhand hold I'd toss the awkward switchblade. The knife would slam into the fence sideways, bounce off and fall in the dead weeds. When I'd get bored with tossing the knife I'd take Missy and walk down the block then around the corner to Julianni's and buy my favorite salami with mustard sandwich on a large French bread roll. Missy and I would take our time walking back home around the block above our house, me feeding pieces of sandwich to Missy, and Missy begging for more salami than bread.

Our neighborhood was quiet except for a sporadic speeding car or a series of cars edging their way up the steep road and I'd thought about the dangers of Missy not being on a leash. She at least stayed by my side on the sidewalk and seldom went into the street unless we crossed it.

Walking up the sidewalk along front of the house along Avalon Avenue, in the center of the front fence, two more extra-wide doors led to an enclosed dirt floor garage that could house two cars. That garage wasn't used and was full of spider webs and discarded junk. None of us wanted to explore the area and we avoided going inside except when we played hide-and-seek.

Further up at the end of the fence was our dirt driveway. The driveway extended about sixty feet long on the upside of the house from the street to dad's workshop in the back. The driveway was wide enough to fit two rows of cars. About ten feet into the driveway was a ten-foot-long wooden ramp that led to our front door. Dad had built the wide ramp to accommodate mom's wheelchair. Between the outside railing on the ramp and the fence along the sidewalk was another parking area that wasn't used except for storing discarded wood and junk to be taken to the dumps. That was where I'd stepped on the rusty nail.

As I wrote before, atop the fence was a three-foot-high sparse railing. I wasn't adventurous, but when I felt brave I'd take to the top planks of the fence, balance myself with the wobbly railing and try to tightrope walk the entire length of the fence, making a turn at the corner of Avalon and Madrid. Most times I was afraid to continue and just sat and straddled then jumped down and landed on the dirt mound inside the fence.

THE FRONT door to our portion of the house was the main entrance to the building. The small entry overhang on our front door shielded the door from rain. The door was heavy wood and the hinges were always oiled. Whenever I'd open the door to go inside Missy would either be standing behind me on the porch or she'd be standing inside waiting for a visitor. Missy owned 402 Avalon, she was present with the family and when she wasn't with us, she was sitting on the porch, lying in the hallway or sitting on the dirt driveway.

Inside the front door was a long, dark twenty feet hallway with a nine-foot-high ceiling. From what I recall the multi-colored linoleum on the floor was scuffed and cracked. I don't recall a light switch on the wall or ceiling light or sconces in the hallway.

Just inside the hall on the left was a doorway that led to mom and dad's bedroom. The door was always closed and sometimes locked. Not that I'd ever tried to open it. Another doorway on the left wall at the end of the hallway led to our big kitchen. On the right side of the hallway inside the front door was a doorway that led to our family room. Down the hallway from the living room was another doorway that led to Joyce and Karen's bedroom. Karen slept on the top bunk.

At the end of the twenty-foot hallway, straight ahead, was the door to the family bathroom in the middle of the house. The room was large and creepy with a toilet to the right of the door and an old fashioned clawfoot bathtub beside that. To the left side inside the bathroom was the medicine cabinet above the sink with two hand towel racks on the wall next to that. Further up the wall at ceiling level was a window about two feet square. On the other side of the wall was the kitchen. That window, which opened inward toward the bathroom, was above the Admiral refrigerator in the kitchen.

Each room in the house was detailed with framed windows and ceiling lights. The colors of the rooms are just a blur to me. Everything about the house, including our furniture was old and musty smelling but at the time I didn't think about old and musty smelling, that was just the way we lived.

Mom and dad's bedroom was always off-limits to us, and the few times I was allowed in there the smell of dad's flannel shirts hung in the air. The odor was dull and unoffending. The room was more masculine than feminine so you knew who wore the pants in the family. Their bed was large, a bedside table sat next to it. A dark wood vanity, a cherry finished wardrobe and two large windows, one in front side of the house and other one in the upside driveway side detailed the rest of their bedroom.

Mt. Davidson 928 feet height near the geographical center of San Francisco

My favorite negative space room without framed photos or paintings hanging on the walls was the living room where the family gathered on Sunday nights across the hall from mom and dad's bedroom. It was adorned with an upright piano, a beat-up, cracked brown leather sofa, an Admiral seventeen-inch television counsel and a large window that overlooked Mt. Davidson across the valley. The 103-foot-tall cross atop Mt. Davidson always intrigued me. The concrete giant was illuminated at night and loomed large into the sky during the daytime. To me the cross was an excellent puzzle. Did the giant contraption represent or reflect religious viewpoints of citizens and politicians, or was the cross a symbol that Jesus was monitoring the City? I liked my idea that Jesus was more than monitoring, he was regulating the City.

The bedroom that Joyce and Karen inhabited was small with one large window. Because of size restriction in the room they slept in bunk beds. Karen was two years my senior, and as a teenager Joyce had eight years on me. Their room always had a feminine fragrance. I knew about girls' menstruating because mom sent me to Jullianni's once a month with a note to purchase their Kotex napkins. This was a chore I'd dreaded.

Across the hallway from Joyce and Karen's bedroom, past the bathroom, and through another doorway was sort of an open entryway to the kitchen. To the left was a second door that led to mom and dad's bedroom. The large kitchen was to the right. Along the doorway wall was a telephone shelf where our black rotary dial telephone was always positioned. Across from that shelf was an area where we stored wood for our free-standing potbelly stove as a heater that had a flat top. One time I'd set fire to the wood pile by accident while playing with matches. Joyce came to the rescue and extinguished the fire with a pot of water. I couldn't tell you how many times that I'd sit on top of the potbelly stove that was usually too hot to sit on, and warm up my little body from the bottom up.

Along the far wall across from the potbelly stove, was a long counter with storage underneath, and with the kitchen sink embedded in the counter. Beside the counter was our clothes washing machine that looked like a white barrel spaceship. A large window was beside the washer that overlooked the upside dirt driveway. Along the opposing wall sat our big black stove, Admiral Refrigerator, some shelves juxtaposed to the Admiral and a built-in nook in the opposing wall. On the top shelf sat mom's Admiral Radio that was usually tuned to a station that played *Hit Parade* songs by balladeer singers like Tony

Bennett, Rosemary Clooney, and Bing Crosby, Nat King Cole, Gisele MacKenzie and the like. I know that visualizing the layout of the kitchen is difficult, but you can try.

One more doorway was across the kitchen, kitty-corner to the hallway door. That doorway led to a tiny room where I slept on the top bunk with Ronnie below. Another small room was next to ours where Timmy slept. Going toward the back of the house a small hallway led into a half-bathroom. The short hallway led down one step into an empty receiving area of about six by eight feet that led to the carriage room. That was dad's workshop. Across that receiving area and one step up dad's cluttered workshop loomed bright. Behind the empty receiving area was a large storage room that dad had built into a rental unit.

That was my living quarters at 402 Avalon Avenue for six short years from 1951 through 1956, but not without reckless abandon.

THE SECOND FLOOR of the house was also off-limits to us. Dad had a large key ring in his private bedroom back in his shop with a multitude of keys on it. The ring hung on a nail on the doorjamb inside his bedroom. The huge set of keys opened every door lock in the house.

When I was eight years old and nobody was around, I'd borrowed dad's keys and snuck around the backside of the house to the door that led to the second floor.

Like a burglar I suspiciously looked around while trying each key in the door lock. That was difficult for a little guy to hold a big flashlight and a large round metal ring with thirty keys, some of which were the old style skeleton keys.

The entrance to the second floor was outside in the center of the house. A couple of trial runs I'd climbed the stairs to the second floor, but quickly returned downstairs. The thought of getting caught with dad's keys and then getting caught on the second floor didn't scare me, the thought of what punishment I'd have to endure did. Mom and dad weren't meanies but I didn't want to find their mean spots. So, with a smile on my little face I'd locked the doors and returned dad's keys, making sure none were out of place.

When the timing was right (that was when dad was at work and my siblings were busy) I'd retrieve the keys and with a flashlight, after unlocking the outside door to the second floor, I'd ascend the squeaky wooden stairs to the second floor and open that door. The hallway between the four one-bedroom apartments upstairs spanned the entire length of the house. The moldy smell of history singed my nose.

The flooring was stiff, just plain wood planks, the ceiling was low and the walls were dried out and splintered under numerous coats of paint. This is my point; everything about the old Brown Farm, the walls, windows, floors, ceilings, lighting fixtures, plumbing and electrical was unsafe, rundown and crumbling. So, why would our parents want to live there? I'd assumed that was because the house was big and the rentals were profitable, that dad had his man-cave in his work shop, that everything wrong with the dwelling could be fixed. The large amount of structural problems had to be fixed, and I knew many of them couldn't be patched or renewed.

THE THIRD FLOOR of the house was the ever-present attic. The steep, narrow, scary stairwell that led to the darkened loft was across the hallway. The eight stairs were rutted and the top rung was missing. I'd have to take a giant step up over the threshold. Another locked door opened into the attic.

Under the light from dad's big flashlight the open spaces looked skeletal with just the wall framing. I took some time scanning the dusty floor and the cobweb rafters. Not wanting to fall through a weak or broken floorboard, I'd tested each board with the tip of my shoe before stepping on it.

Because of the slanted roofline the physical structure could be divided into four small rooms with a hallway down the middle. One little bathroom protruded outward from the roof that had the only window for the entire area. I'd inched my way to the bathroom. The sink, toilet and tub had trashy black stains inside of them. I knew that when blood dried the stain turned black. The sink and tub hadn't been used for decades. Cracks in the window shade where light was defused, created a creepy setting.

Mom had told me that the attic was used for tenant storage. A layer of dust, a couple of discarded and broken turn-of-the-century dressers with drawers and a single pirate's treasure chest that had a large carving of a sailboat on the top, all waited for me to open them.

The dressers didn't interest me. The chest was locked and I wanted to see what was inside, hopefully gold coins worth a million dollars. None of dad's keys opened the lock so I'd guessed that the chest didn't belong to us.

The frightening features about the attic were the creaky noises, the distinct smell of decay and my thought of being locked inside or being caught in there by my family.

I was cautious of my feelings of gloom while I tiptoed about, trying not to make noise. The dangling spider webs from the rafters and framework, sticking to my face stopped me. Angling around the webs and breathing shallowly about any impending doom, I'd remembered overhearing many stories about drifting spirits or ghosts and even ghouls haunted our house. In our living space on the first floor, I'd only heard the floors and walls creaking. Inside the attic space, ideas suffocated me, floating dust crushed my lungs, unknown history of the house shook my nerves and the whiffs of air brushing against me felt like something moving past me.

Was I in a safe place in the attic? Not really. As an eight-year-old, had I exceeded my age responsibilities? I knew I had. Reasons of safety were why mom and dad made the second floor and the attic off-limits. Had I disrespected their rules by breaking into dad's locked bedroom, snatching his keys and flashlight, sneaking upstairs, wanting to break into the treasure chest I'd found in the attic? Yes, I had and my nerves got the better of me.

Something brushed against my flashlight hand and I'd whimpered. Was that my fear of the unexpected? I was scared and sick. Was there a ghost? I'd broken too many parental rules just because of my young curiosity. If I'd just asked mom and dad what was in our attic instead of stealing the time to find out for myself, I wouldn't have been scared or sick.

Making my way back down the splintered narrow stairs to the second floor guided by the flashlight, darting across the hallway thinking that eyes followed me then scurrying down the steep stairs to the outside was an emotional carnage for me. I'd broken my parents trust and launched a sense of misconduct inside me. Within ten minutes I'd become a delinquent.

I locked the door to the stairwell, snuck around the house, making sure nobody had seen me, I'd then entered dad's bedroom and returned the ring of keys and locked his bedroom door.

I wasn't happy about my offense even though over the next two years I'd return to the attic a couple of times with Timmy and Karen. A small level of comfort covered me on those occasions in cohort with my siblings.

The Campbell Kids Gang

LESS A GANG and more misfits, Timmy, Karen and I, somehow were the center of attention in the immediate neighborhood. I was a little kid and a participant in the gang. Timmy and Karen had more friends that were willing to partake in the Campbell Kids quests, which resulted in numerous sporting events on the property around and on 402 Avalon.

As a down-to-earth kid in clothing one size too large, I looked annoyingly poor. I wore 1950s Sears and J.C. Penney fashions (shirts and pants) and not upscale items off of Macy's or Nordstrom clothing racks. My shoes wore out way too often. I recall holes in my soles and tape around my shoes to keep the soles from flapping loose. Mom was constantly darning the heels of my socks and patching the knees on my pants.

About that time in my life a thought drifted inside my brain that I had an idealistic longing for living a brilliant childhood, and what better time to begin that brilliance when I was ten years old.

We offered neighborhood kids admittance into our gang. They didn't seem to mind how I dressed and wanted to join in on the fun. We had no initiation rules to become a Campbell Kids Gang member, yet for the sake of becoming a member, new recruits had to endure some type of initiation, an induction that was pretend yet real, a training session that would reveal any skills the recruits would possess for admittance to gang privileges. Many gang activities took place that I can remember, whether I was privileged to participate in them or not.

We'd planned to hang a new recruit for a joke initiation. Moose Mush was his nickname, a chubby kid about twelve years old who lived a couple of blocks up the hill from us. Six of us stood inside the tall fence in front of the dugout garage. Bobby Elliot was above us on the first floor of the house. He'd devised a noose on one end of a piece of long rope and tied the loose end to the wooden walkway railing.

Moose Mush was willing to have his wrists tied behind his

back and a blindfold placed over his eyes. We balanced a wooden box on top of an old wooden chair. We assisted the boy to stand on top of the box. He was about three feet off the ground.

Bobby threw the noose down to us. The rope had just enough slack to string around the boy's plump neck. The chair wobbled, the boy's chunky legs wobbled, when the legs of the rickety chair collapsed gang members jumped back from the launch of Moose Mush.

The rope that Bobby Eliot tied around the railing gave way and dropped down on top of Moose Mush when he tumbled to the hard ground. He lay stunned. Bobby scrambled around the house and vanished. Karen untied Moose Mush and unleashed the noose from around his neck. While he cried and said he was going to tell on us, Karen said; if you tell on us you can't be a Campbell Kids Gang member.

Moose Mush wasn't seen near our house again.

Another episode was when Timmy built a type of coaster that was about three feet wide and five feet long with four wheels and a free-form front axle that could be steered with rope nailed on the right and left sides. The main problem was how to stop the fast thing while gang members sat around the edges and raced down the steep Avalon Avenue. Our shoes came to the rescue. We had to drag our feet on the pavement to slow and stop the coaster.

Puddin' was the cute button-faced twelve-year-old blonde neighbor who lived across the street from us on Avalon Avenue. She was Karen's friend and so cute that I wanted to be her boyfriend. She had a new pair of white Patent Leather shoes for Sunday school her mother had purchased that Saturday morning. They were tiny and beautiful and shiny and pride gleamed in her eyes over those shoes. Her initial ride on the coaster required that she drag her shoes with the rest of us to help stop the speeding coaster before we came to the intersection of Madrid Street.

We took our assigned seats around the edges of the coaster. I was jubilant to be sitting beside Puddin', she was such a cutie. I recall she smelled like a fresh peach. We raised our feet and cast off, holding onto the edges of the wood and adjusting how we sat. During the first thirty feet the ride was rough like a bicycle with flat tires.

Half way between Edinburgh and Madrid Streets, flying down Avalon Avenue I'd say at least ten miles an hour, our legs were extended straight out so our feet wouldn't drag on the street. Six of us had to apply the brakes, dragging our shoes along the rough asphalt. My imagination saw smoke billowing from the bottoms of our shoes as we applied pressure on our leather soles to stop the wooden carriage.

The uproar of our laughter, the clatter of the coaster's wheels on the asphalt, the bouncing of the coaster, the gusts of wind in our faces and the sheer joy of freedom almost buried the frightening screams from Puddin'. My new shoes, my new shoes, she yelled, while like the rest of us, she gripped the edges of the coaster for support, and applied pressure to the bottom of her shoes.

With consorted effort from our strong legs and knowing that a car might plow into the coaster that would send us to heaven, we stopped the cart at the stop sign. Laughing and screaming, we'd realized the pleasure of fear and destiny. Puddin' sat whimpering and held one shoe up and showed us what remained. The heel was gone and the sole was hot with a large hole in the center.

The damsel I wanted to be my girlfriend but couldn't be because she was two years my elder, the adorable Puddin', put her shoe on and ran home crying. A couple of weeks later her brother Brian confessed to me that she was forbidden by their mother to ever play with the Campbell kids again.

My idea of a future romance and marriage with Puddin' had ended.

Other adolescent and somewhat juvenile pastimes became event fixtures for us. Dad built me a pair of walking stilts that hefted up a foot higher than my 4 feet 8 inches. I still have scars on my knees and elbows that prove that I'd fallen off them dozens of times.

From dad's excellent woodworking skills, he manufactured wooden rifles and pistols and stapled rubber bands on the front of the barrels for us to shoot pebbles at paper targets in the backyard. The triggers on the insignificant weapons were wooden clothespins attached on the top backsides of the guns. To heck with targets drawn on paper and nailed to the back fence. Our real targets were cars driving by the empty lot. Bobby Harnwell, Richard Patoni and I would hide in the tall weeds, wrap a bent nail around the rubber band, pull the nail back and hold it in place with the clothespin. When a car drove past us we'd aim and shoot, hoping to hit the car.

One time I was by myself hiding in the tall weeds in the empty lot, I'd aimed my toy gun at a slow moving black Ford, released the bent nail from the clothes pin and the nail hit the car. The Ford stopped within a few feet. I panicked and rolled down the hillside concealed under the two-foot-tall weeds. At the bottom of the empty lot I dropped my toy pistol under the weeds and ran down Lisbon Street alongside the front of Monroe Elementary School, turned right on Excelsior Avenue and ran another three blocks to the busy Mission Street.

Out of breath, I knew I wouldn't get captured but I'd performed another misdeed and was ashamed. Wandering around Mission Street for an hour I felt guilt and shame and decided that causing damage wasn't worth the ugly emotions. Without childhood guidance from responsible adults, like in *Lord of the Flies*, the descent into savagery has no limits and that the real beast of humanity is inside all of us.

What interested me most about my childhood, and which I didn't know how to pursue, I needed to know the reasons behind layered silence that inhibited my family, and why that silence restricted me from asking my parents questions about anything; about who my grandparents were, was my dad adopted, why did we live at 402 Avalon and not in a regular house?

A few answers came to the many introverted questions I'd thought about while playing in the empty lot across the street. I dug caves in the soft dirt, rode down the dried weeded hillside on top of big pieces of cardboard, had sod fights with Bobby Harnwell, and understood that playtime was best instead of worrying why my parents were different from my friends' parents, why we lived in a haunted house and why my friends were either afraid to come and play at the house or were forbidden to play with me.

The empty lot provided solace to my convoluted childhood emotions. The open space where Missy was my mascot, my imagination devised future projects. I was a subject of being isolated during a decade when family communications were constrained and I was a kid who needed to discover confidence, acceptance and permission to understand who I was.

THE CAMPBELL KIDS GANG was just a vessel of silly events during weekend days over periods of time when mom didn't take us to the special places throughout the City. Ocean Beach along the Great Highway, Playland, and the Cliff house, Fleishhacker Zoo, Golden Gate Park, Fisherman's Wharf and Aquatic Park were just a few special places she took us to. She loved driving around Twin Peaks and down the twisted Lombard Street. Mom had an essential freedom while driving. Her rheumatoid arthritis directed her future with insurmountable pain, yet while she was driving the pain was gone.

The Campbell Kids activities on weekend days were cut short when mom wanted to go places. She'd drive us out to the Great Highway where we'd hike around the Cliff House, look down upon and admire the privately-owned swimming pool complex of Sutro Baths. We'd then go down to the long Ocean Beach that fronted Playland.

Looking out over the Pacific Ocean afforded me some time to consider how big the world was. The ocean water was always too cold to swim in. I'd just wade in the foamy surf and enjoy the rough sand that gathered around my feet. Missy came with us and divided her time by slopping along the foamy surf and rolling in the warm sand.

Weather at the beach was sometimes overcast or foggy and cold, but we didn't let any condition deter our fun. Mom would wait in the car for us while we took off our socks and shoes, rolled up our trousers over our knees and waded in the surf. After finding pebbles and small sand dollars we'd toss them, trying to skim them across the surface.

When our fingers and faces got numb we'd return to the car. Before letting Missy inside the car I'd have to brush as much sand out of her thick fur with my hands. She loved the attention and would help me by wagging her tail and by rolling on the asphalt.

Cliff House 1955

All the clean, fresh ocean air shot youthful adrenalin through my veins and I was ready to play real-life. The most fun place on earth during the 1950s was Playland at the beach. When mom would embrace us with a trip to Playland, Karen and I would run around like best friends. Timmy would go his own way and sometimes we wouldn't reconnect until meeting back at the car.

The combined fragrances of pink cotton candy, corn dogs, candied apples and Mexican cuisine filled our noses. The clamor from the traffic and by the various rides and attractions elevated our vigor.

Mom would give us a couple of dollars and we'd run off to play. She would then buy a coffee and two enchiladas for herself at the Mexican Kiosk, smother them with chopped onions, get back in her car and park facing toward the Pacific Ocean, eat and wait for us to return.

The physical torture of riding the Big Dipper, Tilt-a-Whirl, the Octopus, bumper cars, Fly-O-Plane, Carousel and a few other rides for ten cents was phenomenal. The Penny Arcade was mundane and the gaming skills so routine, instead, we couldn't run fast enough between rides. And then we couldn't wait for a ride to stop so we could get on another ride. The juvenile energy combined with the crowds of people and the gobbling down of pink cotton candy added to our excitement.

Playland at the Beach 1955

The twenty-five-cent entry into the Fun House was our place of leisure, and I'd considered that building a charming, fun torture chamber. Karen and I would pay the entry fee and spend at least two hours injuring our bodies on the rides.

We'd start riding the human roulette wheel known to me as the giant turntable. The large flat surface was sloped around the outer edges. Thirty or so riders would scoot to the center of the round turntable and sit back-to-back before it started turning. Spinning was slow at first then accelerate faster for at least two minutes until the inertia of centrifugal force slid all riders off.

The object was to be the last person on the turntable that skidded across the ten-foot surface and landed on the floor around the perimeter. And, if a rider was lucky, slam into the padded wall head first.

When I was eight years old and ready to spin longer than anyone, the turntable started too quickly and I was jolted to my left side, the turntable spun clockwise, and I fell on my face and skidded across the entire surface, leaving half the skin on my left cheek smeared on the slick turntable wood. That injury didn't stop me from having fun though.

Karen and I would disappear into the mirrored corridor where our bodies looked distorted in configured full-length mirrors, squeezing our bent reflections into Humpty Dumpty kids, or fat midgets, and our twisted faces resembled Dr.

Frankenstein's monster.

Playland Fun House 1955

Twenty times we'd ride down the six metal slides on burlap bags, screaming the entire length on the slick surface with multiple humps along the forty-foot length. Our legs would cramp from running up the steps to the top of the slides but we didn't care, the exhilaration for the bumpy ride and the journey was what mattered.

We'd try to balance while walking over the fifteen-foot crooked bridge that would wobble and rise and fall then wobble more, making us fall to our knees. We'd scramble to the other side and swear we never try that again, and then we'd wait in line to attack the rigged bridge again and again.

The giant rotating barrel was one huge challenge. The barrel rotated at various speeds and I'd fall inside, tumble, bang up my head, scrape my palms and get stepped on by other uncoordinated adults and kids. After I'd crawl my way out the other end I'd start over and over again until I'd only stumble, not fall and walk through the barrel, stepping over smaller kids that fell inside and couldn't get up.

Time flew by as we laughed from exhaustion, the feeling that zaps youthful energy, but doesn't discourage the need to start afresh. We'd exit the Fun House and purchase corn dogs, sodas and sit and eat and laugh.

MANY FEATURES to see and do in San Francisco during the 1950s remain now. The big difference between then and now was childhood innocence. Everything was new to the Campbell Kids Gang, and as the years flew by and we continued to visit the same places over and over, the exciting freshness continued inside us. Mom would gather us up, stuff us in her car and start driving.

San Francisco and Golden Gate Park

We must have visited Fleishhacker Zoo over ten times, which now is the San Francisco Zoo. We swam in Fleishhacker Pool at least ten times, the largest heated outdoor salt water swimming pool in the world. That pool remained open for more than four decades until its closure in 1971. I know we visited Golden Gate Park at least ten times over six years. The fine arts at De Young Museum always pulled my attention. The serenity of the five acre Japanize Tea Garden with the Drum Bridge and the tea house kept me calm. The Conservatory of Flowers made mom happy. I loved the paddleboats in the Stow and Spreckels Lake. The Dutch and Murphy windmills in Golden Gate Park fascinated me. They were restored and add to the flavor of San Francisco.

The zoo was an indispensable part of the City. The animals were well fed and healthy. Excited monkeys in their cages were one of the most fascinating exhibitions. They would beg for food by extending their arms through the bars. Some monkeys would sit and look bored and others would spit at gawkers or throw bowls of water at them.

When we went to the zoo on weekends I'd push mom in her wheelchair, maneuvering her around crowds of people. I thought that everybody in San Francisco was at the zoo. Mom would purchase peanuts in the shell to throw to the elephants and monkeys. The fragrance of the eucalyptus trees combined with animal feces, salty air, screaming kids, reprimanding adults, frantic zoo keepers and Karen nagging that she wanted to go home, was all too shattering to my youth. I wanted to be where the animals were. After all, that was where Tarzan was so why couldn't I be living with the animals?

Fleishhacker Pool

In Golden Gate Park there is the Music Concourse area, the sunken, oval-shaped open-air plaza that was originally excavated for the California Midwinter International Exposition of 1894. That fresh-air outdoor stage is where numerous music performances have enlightened San Francisco citizens throughout the decades.

Mom loved driving through the park. The sights and smells reminded her of the countryside around her hometown of Butler, Pennsylvania. We'd picnic on the Park's greens and toss a tennis ball. When we took Missy with us, she would run and dodge us when we chased her, but she wouldn't fetch the tennis ball.

Mom loved taking us to a beach. Any beach was fine with her. A few times she'd driven us to Half Moon Bay beach where we'd picnic and play the entire day. Mostly though, we'd go to either San Francisco's Ocean Beach on the Great Highway or to the small beach at Aquatic Park across the street from Ghirardelli Square to splash and play in the surf.

One Saturday mom drove us to San Mateo Memorial Park for a picnic. Mom's friend Mr. Bertha Webb with her two kids Gordon and June, who were my age, met us there. We slopped around in the creek the entire day after eating grilled hamburgers. The best thing about that picnic was the coal roasted corn-on-the-cob, and of course the root beer soda.

A few of these outings we'd brought along Timmy's schoolmate Bobby Elliot, and when Joyce wanted to go she'd bring her schoolmate Jackie Elliot, Bobby's older sister. One summer vacation we'd taken Jackie and Bobby with us to Oroville. While there, for entertainment, mom would take us to swim in Feather River where Joyce and Jackie would check out the older boys. Mom would also take us to a drive-in movie. Riding our bicycles around the countryside was our main activity and stopping to swim in a deep-water hole. The Elliots were our devoted neighbors that lived across Avalon Avenue down the block a few houses.

Bobby was the comedic topic of many conversations in our family, how his mother was always drunk, would hang out of their second floor living room window late afternoons facing Avalon Avenue, look at 402 Avalon and call Bobby to come home. She had a deep smoker's voice, gravelly yet clear, something like Janis Joplin combined with Joe Cocker.

Bobby told us that she put hot oil in his shoes when he was getting dressed to go to school. Another time she threw a fork at him when he was jumping down their stairs to go to school and the fork stuck in his back. Why she treated Bobby wrongly I felt was because of her drinking problem, any other problems she might have had were never mentioned by Bobby.

Some school days Timmy and Bobby would walk together to Denman Junior High and later after junior high graduation, the following school year they'd walk to Balboa High School. Bobby was a Campbell Kids Gang member and much of an irritation to me, always trying to confuse me, he'd even turn the charm on for mom, just like I said, he was the *Eddie Haskell*, neighborhood dupe from the *Leave It to Beaver* television show.

Mom loved to go to the Geneva Drive-in. Kids admission was free and the drive-in was inexpensive entertainment. Mom would just jam us in the backseat of her car with bags of popcorn and bottles of soda. We'd eat and fall asleep before the second movie was over.

Dad was busy on weekends, but under pressure from mom he'd take us to the El Rey movie theater on Ocean Avenue whenever a new Francis the Talking Mule movie premiered. I think we'd seen all seven of the Francis movies with dad.

El Rey Movie Theater on Ocean Avenue

My favorite past-time on Saturdays was going to the Granada Theater matinée to see science-fiction movies. Either Karen and I or all three of us, Timmy, Karen and I went to watch and be scared from movies such as, The *Day the Earth Stood Still, Forbidden Planet, It Came from Outer Space, When Worlds Collide, Flight to Mars, The Thing, This Island Earth, Creature from the Black Lagoon, Them, Tarantula*. I wanted to watch the two or three cartoons the theater would show before the start of the scary movies, cartoons that featured *Wile E. Coyote, Bugs Bunny, Porky Pig, Elmer Fudd, Foghorn Leghorn, Yosemite Sam, Pepé Le Pew, Casper the Ghost* and many others. Karen was annoyed from the cartoons. She just wanted the movies to start. That was Karen; no fooling around, get to the main subject and be done with it.

Granada Movie Theater on Mission Street

As I'd mentioned at the beginning of this section, the Campbell Kids Gang was much less of a gang and consisted more of neighborhood misfit kids, searching for something useful and entertaining to do other than to just complete household chores, watch television and play cards with our parents. As the new dissident generation, the kids that would rebel against a century of established cultural customs, domestic traditions, societal practices and ethical behaviors; we became the Rebels without causes.

Karen & Benny

I WAS ten when my twelve-year-old sister told me she was going to kill me.

While you're asleep, Benny, Karen said, I'm going to stab you in the heart with Ronnie's hunting knife.

She sat on the kitchen floor in front of me in her multicolored striped socks, half-sleeved green frock, stoop shoulders underneath her pageboy haircut and adept hands peeling potatoes.

My knees played knock-knock after her statement that she was going to stab me.

I'm telling mom, I said, you can't kill me because I'm your little brother.

Humorless, squinting eyes stared at me. If you tell mom, she said, I'm *really* going to kill you. She'll think that Ronnie stabbed you.

Ronnie was our Nazi brother who was ten years older than me. He pictured himself as the Dalai Lama, a spiritual teacher who enlightened others, and not a real Nazi, but a superior person that had a right to dominate others, just as he professed to me.

He had one weapon in his bedroom that I played with when he wasn't home. The item was an eight-inch western hunting knife with a stained leather handle and a ratty leather sheath.

Ronnie said he found the knife in the basement. I believed him because I'd found much more in the basement than an antique hunting knife.

He kept the knife in the top drawer of his dresser, underneath his socks. I was happy he didn't wear underpants because he'd have hidden the knife under them and I wouldn't want to touch them. When he wasn't home I'd sneak in his room and slide my belt through the slit in the sheath and carry the knife around underneath my shirttail. The knife was dull. Yet, a few times I'd retrieved Band-Aids from the bathroom cabinet to cover small finger cuts.

When Karen said she'd stab me in the heart with that knife, I giggled, recalling Bugs Bunny and Daffy Duck cartoons at the Granada Theater on Mission Street. Their antics were just as violent as Karen's words. She couldn't kill me, she could scarcely see through the magnifying eye glasses she wore all the time. Besides, she was experiencing pre-menstrual cycle syndrome. Whatever that was my ten-year-old mind didn't understand. As usual, she was trying to find her voice, ways of expressing her love and gratitude to me as my sister and a Campbell family member.

Karen and I were in the large kitchen with our legs folded underneath us. The cracked vinyl floor had interlaced squares with black, white and blue borders. The designs were visually irritating and we had to live with them.

Mom had me mop the floor at least once a month with a tin bucket half-full of hot water and detergent and a deck mop with a hardwood handle. The vinyl looked dirty all the time so keeping the floor clean was easy, yet dust and dirt from our driveway and ashes from the potbelly stove was an everyday occurrence.

Listen to me, Benny, Karen said. I always win playing checkers. I run faster, skate faster, I'm taller than you and I'm two years older. If I want to kill you I'll kill you.

You won't kill me, I said.

Why won't I kill you?

Because you wear glasses, you can't see me and because I'm invisible.

That's stupid, she said. That's another thing I have on you. You're stupid and I'm not.

You're not stupid because you have nothing to think about.

Accidents happen, Karen said, and one might happen to you.

We'd just finished peeling ten Russet potatoes. The skins were in a pyramid we'd piled on top of the Sunday Examiner comics that was spread between us. The peeled potatoes were atop pieces of wax paper. The deep fryer, with boiling Crisco oil was waiting on top of the stove for the basket plunge of raw French-cut potatoes.

We loved French fires so much that mom purchased us a

French fry cutter. There were two stainless steel cutting blades. One was for regular fries and one for shoestring fries. Karen put one potato in the cutter and pushed the handle. Potato pieces long and thick came out the other side ready for the fryer.

You see, she said, her sad magnified eyes digging at my soul. It's like this. I plunge Ronnie's hunting knife in your heart just like I pushed this potato through the cutting blade. Then you're dead. Maybe I'll kill you tonight.

You can't kill me with the knife, I said, my blood will stain the sheets.

Karen's swollen eyes tilted at me. Then I'll shove a stick of dynamite up your ass and light the fuse.

I'm telling mom you swore at me, I said.

Composed in her cross-legged slouch she didn't hesitate. If you tell mom I'll kill you.

I shuffled on my knees. You can't kill me twice.

I can kill you as many times as I want.

Karen wasn't a threat. Sometimes her dark side was vile, cunning and suspicious, as a twelve-year-old could be. Where would she get a stick of dynamite anyway? My butt was too small for her to shove dynamite into it.

Think about this, she said. Don't be worried if you don't wake up in the morning.

I can't worry if I don't wake up after being killed, I said. Waking up dead was for zombies and I'm just a kid.

Yeah? Karen questioned. If I don't kill you, mom will run you over with her wheelchair and you'll be dead anyway.

Mom's wheelchair is too small to run over me.

Karen put another potato through the cutter. Her menacing attitude had turned into a guttural laugh. I then started gathering up the cut potatoes for the fryer.

If I don't kill you tonight, she said, I'll kill you tomorrow night.

I folded up the newspaper with the peeled potato skins inside, bent the edges over then rolled the paper into the shape of a dough rolling pin. Karen put another potato in the French fry cutter and began the process again.

I'm just kidding, she said, if I wanted to kill you, you'd be dead already.

That was the way Karen communicated with me, her youthful Patti Page face threatening to murder me, or cutting off my penis, maybe even shaving my head while I slept, perhaps piling up my clothes in the driveway and lighting them on fire among other intimidations that would challenge my mindset. Her threats to me were constant and I'd often wondered how she interacted with her friends at school. Was she a threat to them or did she treat me as an inferior rival?

Karen was a crusader and I was her victim. I wasn't afraid of her most of the time because I'd understood that being serious was her form of comedy, and she wouldn't commit heinous crimes against her sweetheart younger brother. However, her large magnified eyes behind her glasses always scared me.

There were a couple of years when Karen and I were a cohesively sister and brother, laughing and joking while playing cards and dominos, learning to roller stake together, attending Sunday School at the local Baptist Church on Ocean Avenue, playing together at Playland, cooking pancakes and eggs for breakfast and even having fun sod fights in the empty lot. When Karen was twelve years old something had changed inside her, whether it was the onset of puberty, gender differences or family controversies, our sister brother relationship weakened and she distanced herself from me.

Treasure

SUNDAY OCTOBER 2, 1955 was a weary day for teenagers and rebels around the world. James Dean, the young twenty-four-year-old actor had died in an auto accident two days previous. His death was a minor disruption for me as a ten-year-old. I didn't know what rebellion meant, least a youthful societal rebellion against the establishment or the Man. My father was the Man and 402 Avalon was my establishment. He purchased the house and I was living in it.

Ronnie's birthday was October 3rd. His youthful Albert Einstein appearance had ten years of separation between us. That meant we had nothing in common except that he considered himself my watchdog, my gatekeeper, the one adult my mom commissioned to punish me for any misconduct. He thought he was my savior. I knew he was the devil. Our brotherly relationship was compromised via age difference and behavioral psychology. Violence wasn't his forte, nevertheless he liked to vice grip my shoulders and shake me into confessing whatever secret transgressions I'd performed. He was certain I had many, but I only had one.

While in the kitchen one Saturday afternoon, Ronnie restrained me by my shoulders and made me stand in front of him while he sat in a chair.

His evil stare didn't scare me when he started asking me questions. Where did you get the tobacco bag of coins I found in your drawer? There's at least three dollars in quarters dines and nickels in there.

I can't tell you it's my secret, I said.

Did you steal one of dad's tobacco bags to put the coins in?

I didn't steal anything, I said, empty tobacco bags are all over the house.

Tell me the truth, he said. I'm keeping the coins until you tell me that you stole the money.

You can't keep the money because finders keepers, losers weepers.

His vice grip hurt my shoulders while he shook me back and forth. I was a rag doll and he shook me again then pushed me to the floor. You have to stay in your room, he said, until you tell me the truth.

I felt like he just kicked me in the gut and slapped me across the face. I stood up off the floor and backed away. His evil eyes followed me. He dangled my bag of coins overhead. I ran for my room and snuck down the hallway through the back door and into dad's workshop. He could keep the bag of money because I'd get more and hide that where he wouldn't find it.

Going outside in the backyard with my Mr. Potato Head was the best diversion. I wished I could have reconstructed Ronnie's ears, eyes, nose and a mouth upside down, like I'd done to Mr. Potato Head.

The coins came from my treasure find buried in the dirt under the house. The unfinished garage that was dug out from the hillside was just a vacant cave of mounds of hard dirt on one side. I played there with my toy dump truck. The overhead, dangling light was dim, but I'd discovered the buried coin treasure just before Christmas 1955, when I was in the sixth grade, and one month before Ronnie found my tobacco bag full of the coins inside one of my socks in my dresser drawer.

While digging in the hard dirt with dad's long neck screwdriver, making a trail to accommodate my toy truck, the screwdriver hit a hard object. That metallic object was a silver dollar. I picked up the coin, brushed off the dirt. Goose bumps rose on my arms. A blanket of heat gushed through my body. I'd found a silver dollar buried in the dirt. I wiped the coin clean with the tail of my shirt and examined it under the dim light. A shadow brushed across my hand and even though I was by myself, I wasn't alone.

Mom and dad used silver dollars to pay for groceries and other things. They were commonly used back in the day and I'd seen them but never handled one. I would have to wash the coin to see the full beauty. Would I tell anyone about my find? I wouldn't tell anyone that I'd found a silver dollar in the basement. I picked up the screwdriver again and dug in a circle where the coin was buried. Nickels, dimes and quarters appeared. I picked them up one at a time, wiped them off and put them in my pants pocket.

Digging for more coins was my tiniest problem, keeping the money a secret was the biggest magic of all. Could I make this my secret? Could I be the Captain Hook and not let Ronnie be the crocodile that would snap off my hand? I wasn't a bad kid like Captain James Hook was, the lord of the pirate village of Neverland. I was just a neglected kid that had to discover my own way.

I'd seldom had money except for a quarter that mom would give me to go to a movie or a nickel to buy one chocolate covered donut at the bakery and eat it while walking home.

As I dug a few coins out of the dirt that amounted to two dollars, I'd decided not to uncover any more coins at that time. There had to be more buried coins deep down and I wanted to be surprised with discovering them. Washing the ones, I'd found, counting and hiding them would be my first concerns. I found a large rock and put it on top of my treasure mound and brushed dirt, half covering the rock. I'd memorized the location of the mound and would return many times.

I wouldn't tell anyone about my find, not even Karen, because she'd tell everyone about my secret, not allowing me to have anything of my own. Or, she would kill me and get the money for herself.

My secret was safe with me and from Christmas time 1955 and forward, I had plenty of extra change.

About once a month, treating Bobby Harnwell to horseback riding in John McLaren Park was my pleasure. The cost was a dollar fifty an hour for each of us. The park was a quarter mile up the hill from our house on Avalon Avenue. A riding stable with trails throughout the park's 317 acres made for excellent riding. This park was the second largest in San Francisco besides Golden Gate Park. Bobby and I were natural cowboys riding around hillsides without a care in the world.

We hated when the hour was over and we had to return our favorite horses to the stables. I'd named my horse Silver after the Lone Ranger's, and Bobby named his Trigger after Roy Roger's horse. They were fast and ran like racing horses.

Whenever I needed money I'd go digging for more coins, wash them and bag a dollar or two. I had two new problems;

hiding my digging spot in the dirt and making sure that I wasn't followed to the garage when I'd go digging for more coins. What didn't pop into my mind was when and why the coins were buried. Coins were dated for the 1940s and a few of the Indian head pennies were from the turn of the century, but their ages didn't stop me from using them.

Never telling anybody about my buried treasure had benefits. All the extra money came in handy during my last year living at 402 Avalon Avenue.

CHRISTMAS WAS less than three months away. Preparing for my first Christmas knowing that Santa Clause wasn't real was nauseating to me. What good was the holiday without the big, fat white bearded white man in a red suit, flying around the world on a sleigh powered by reindeer, magically carrying enough gifts for everybody?

I knew that mom, dad and brothers and sisters lied to me, little white lies that weren't important, but were important, things that I should believe in like the Tooth Fairy lives, Halloween ghosts are real, personal angels look over you, and Easter rabbits laying boiled eggs, and Santa Clause in charge of a horde of slave labor elves and ever-energized reindeer. One reindeer in particular had a red nose? What was I to do with false knowledge that was real but not real, become a successful fairytale salesman?

I'd saved my weekly allowance and with digging up coins over the past few months, I'd decided to purchase mom a coffee warmer as a Christmas gift. The cost was fourteen dollars, a fortune during that time.

Mom loved drinking black coffee and always had a steaming percolator on the stove. The burning odor from the coffee singed my nose. I'd circumvent that by gifting the coffee warmer. There would be no more flames under the percolator, just an electric heating element that wouldn't burn the coffee.

My upcoming eleventh birthday would be on January 17, 1956, and if I'd lived beyond that date without spending all the coins in my secret bank in the garage and Karen killing me, that would be a landmark in my life. So, maintaining best behavior was my constant. I'd hoped mom and dad would gift me a red Schwinn 3-speed bicycle for my birthday, a Daisy BB rifle, a pair of Levi jeans and also ankle leather boots. I knew that a Schwinn bicycle was too expensive, as were the leather boots. As for the Daisy BB rifle, mom wasn't against guns, but even a BB rifle in the city wasn't an awful idea. I'd have to settle for jeans and maybe a bone to feed Missy.

One afternoon after I'd begged mom for all those gifts, she said they couldn't afford any of them. If those gifts weren't forthcoming I'd have to settle by playing with Ronnie's western hunting knife, pretending to kill the enemy army and cut my little fingers by misuse. I'd already put my right fist through our living room window because Timmy and Karen had locked me out of the house. The lengthy jagged scar along my hypothenar, the fleshy eminence along the side of my right palm, proved that bleeding to death at the time wasn't my fate.

Timmy was four years older than me. He seemed to shuffle around a lot. After all, James Dean was dead, the actor who was supposed to liberate the troubled new generation of teens and young adults, freeing them from inherited social enigmas, burying the redundant, obsolete ideals of gender inequalities and sexual restrictions. Individuality and liberation were the new rules for the younger generation. Little did they know that the older generation controlled everything.

Like any of the liberations were going to happen for society let alone the Campbell kids.

Timmy and I communicated on levels of physicality. We had tickling fights, shoulder punching and pushing maneuvers. We watched television and slept inside the same house and ate Sunday family dinners together. Outside the house we had different friends and interests. Except for when Timmy, Karen and I adopted the names Snap, Crackle and Pop after Kellogg's breakfast cereal Rice Krispies gnomic characters. I never knew which one of us was which character. We'd just reel off the names like they were ours and laugh about it.

We'd also made up a Campbell Kids song that went like this:

Sa-sa-pa pop-a-sue,

hi-goodbye-soup-pie,
basu-and-pasu,
Dagwood-ear-naked-tree-er.

The song had zero meaning. The Campbell kids' form of communication was at least, sensitive to our own emotions. What did we have if we couldn't communicate effectively with each other?

When Timmy's youthful appearance of the actor Gilbert Roland stared at me I knew he was going to start a tickle fight, and I'd always fall on the floor and yell for mercy. If Karen was around she'd jump on top of me and help Timmy by holding me down and they'd both tickle me until I'd wildly fling my arms and legs.

My middle sister Joyce had a little over eight years of maturity on me. Just because your eighteen years old doesn't mean you're a woman, I'd overheard dad say. She knew otherwise. For a while I had to share a bed with her for some unknown reason. She'd come home late at night, pull me from a deep sleep and search inside my underpants for flees. Prodding my young genitals seemed unnecessary while she searched for flees. I knew girls were silly and being so insistent with tickling my privates was senseless to me. After a week of that I'd decided to stay clear of girls, especially eighteen-year old girls.

Joyce's youthful Judy Garland appearance drastically changed with her butch haircut and penciled-in eyebrows. Her Garland look ended as did her dwindling sugary personality. Betty Boop was her newest guise. I didn't mind the change until she started dressing in men's shirts and jeans and hanging with motorcycle gang members. Of course, that was exciting to me since Marlon Brando was the new biker dude in the movies, rebelling against the man in the movie *The Wild One*. I lived in a separate world from Joyce, me in my kid phase, she in her rebellious teenage stage.

Every Sunday mom was in her wheelchair in the kitchen late afternoons preparing dinner for the whole family. Her delicious pot roast with whole carrots, onions, celery and potatoes and giblet gravy was sometimes on the menu, and when it was, the scrumptious fragrance that filled the house was to die for. Like playing her accordion, her excellent cooking ability was another gift. The rheumatoid arthritic condition deforming every joint in her body didn't curtail those gifts. However, the arthritis did inhibit her mothering abilities.

MinAleta Campbell was a high school graduate from Butler, Pennsylvania. She birthed six children before she was thirty years old. She weathered the drive across the continent in an old jalopy from Pittsburgh, Pennsylvania, to San Francisco, California, while persistent rheumatoid arthritis invaded her body. She was in the process of raising her children, comforting her husband, all the while being tortured with that unrelenting disease.

A few medical specialists in San Francisco suggested specific dietary and exercise programs for the crippling disease, like eating raw liver and performing squats at the kitchen sink if she could stand up. They gave her therapeutic massages and swimming as exercise. They experimented with new pharmaceuticals, injecting drugs into her shoulders, hips and knees. Her doctor suggested surgeries to straighten her knees. He prescribed knee and leg braces for her daily use. Articles were written about mom and photos were taken during medical rehab swimming, and then they were posted in the San Francisco Examiner in 1954. She was interviewed and sometimes hounded by newspaper reporters. She loved the attention but didn't want the hoopla it generated.

Mom was an ordinary woman suffering impossible pain, crying at night in bed behind her closed door while muscles ached, knees, hips, fingers, wrists, elbows and shoulders twisted and deformed. She cried while under doctor's care and supervision as her body transformed from a normal woman who could walk and perform daily function, into a suffering cripple. She'd adjusted her attitude as best she knew how but hated having to live a crippled life.

On my eleventh birthday on January 17, 1956, while sitting alone on the wooden bench in the kitchen nook, facing my birthday cake mom had baked, she looked so little sitting in her wheelchair. As a small woman of 5' 2", she struggled to hold her black Kodak box camera between her deformed fingers, focusing the lens on me. I realized just how extraordinary and beautiful mom was.

She said, say cheese, I smiled and she snapped the photo.

Nice one, she said, and put the camera on her lap. Again, at the wondrous moment of turning eleven years old with just mom and me together, I understood that I loved her, a word that would never be exchanged between us, but we both felt that mother/son endearing love.

My 11th Birthday January 17, 1956

We shared a piece of cake because we needed to save some for the rest of the family. We talked about what I enjoyed most about school. I took a clearer look at mom. Her arthritic condition added at least ten years to her appearance.

She wasn't yet confined to a wheelchair, but she spent most of her time navigating around the house in it. With dark hair and deep eyes, she resembled a youthful Elizabeth Taylor. At forty years old her muscles had atrophied. She was already over-the-hill plump. What she did well was whip through the house like hell-on-wheels, yelling at us kids when we did something wrong like bouncing a golf ball off the hallway walls, playing tag you're it in the house, or chasing each other with Ronnie's western hunting knife.

Caring about any of that while sharing the piece of cake was futile. I relished that special birthday time with mom.

Doggie Diner

MOST OF the time on Saturdays and Sundays dad was in his workshop, navigating around his stock of current machines; freestanding drill press, Craftsman professional table saw, Acetylene welding gas cylinder and equipment, gas lawnmower engines, electric motors and all kinds of hand tools and building materials. Special building projects used most of his free time. When he wasn't working he napped in his locked bedroom, which was forbidden for any of us to enter.

Little did he know?

Dad was a high school graduate and his job at Southern Pacific Railroad in South San Francisco utilized his special carpentry, plumbing and electric skills as a railroad car inspector. When the Bethlehem Steel job ended after WWII, he worked double-shifts at the railroad. He still had two jobs yet one employer and his time was limited at home.

Along with working and designing and inventing products like electric lawn mowers and an electric wheelchair, dad had purchased a diner in South San Francisco across the El Camino Real road from the Southern Pacific Railroad yards where he'd worked. The restaurant was a typical 1950s diner that was long and narrow inside, with a neon sign outside, eight small booths to the left when you entered, a bathroom in the back, maybe eight stools at the long Formica counter on the right side, stainless steel panels on the wall behind the stove, clear cake and pie containers along the counter, a tiered candy display on the counter near the front door by the cash register.

The menu was typical diner cuisine; waffles, pancakes, eggs, hash browns and bacon and French toast for breakfast; hamburgers, French fries, club sandwiches, hotdogs and chili for lunch; ham, chicken, patty melts, roast beef, country fried steak, biscuits and gravy and baked beans for dinner. And, don't forget about the coffee that was ongoing.

He may have owned the Doggie Diner for a year or so. Toward the end of dad's ownership, he would take Timmy,

Karen and I there on Sunday nights to help wash the front windows, mop the floors, disinfect the booths and counter and scrub the flat surface of the stove. As payment he'd give each of us our choice of a candy bar like 3Muskateers or Snickers or Milky Way or a bag of M&M'^{s} or a bag of Planter's Peanuts. We didn't mind minimum candy wage. I was ecstatic about the labor payment because I had all the coins I needed.

The first scuttlebutt between mom and dad was that the main waitress at the Doggie Diner was pilfering ham and roasts and other essential food items, which cut into the profits and created inventory problems. The second scuttlebutt between them was that dad was having an affair with that main waitress at the diner. She was quite pretty in the typical waitress apparel from that time, and her makeup and piled hair was for the pleasure of the customers—my dad, too.

Mom argued with dad about that tall, skinny harlot who was managing, cooking, wore too much red lipstick and who was waiting on customers, wiggling her rear and dipping forward to show off her melons that were just small lemons. The third scuttlebutt was that dad found extra time and worked at the diner cooking, flirting and encouraging that harlot to be merciful with customers. He'd even give hamburgers and chili dinners to tramps, vagabonds and hobos that hobbled into the diner for free handouts. Dad was that generous and I'd seen him tell a homeless man not to worry about paying.

Arguments between mom and dad over the burdensome Doggie Diner were done. No more arguments and no more Doggie Diner. Dad had to dump the eatery and move on to more prosperous ventures. He also had to give up the winsome harlot who thought she was Greta Garbo.

Fire her for pilfering hams, the Lord knows she had two below her knees she called calves, mom said.

The next Sunday's dinner at home included a serious offer and critical discussion between Dad, Ronnie and Joyce. Mom had cooked a delicious roast and was in her wheelchair pulling the sweet-smelling food out of the oven. I watched her, starving from playing outside all day and digging up another dollar in coins from the dirt in the garage.

Dad stood in the middle of the large kitchen wearing his

red and black flannel shirt, Big Ben trousers and work shoes, looking imposing. Ronnie and Joyce faced him looking less than mediocre. The smile across dad's face was a one-hundred-watt light bulb. Joyce and Ronnie expressions were like cattle being led to slaughter.

Your mother and I decided that the two of you should take over ownership of the Doggie Diner, dad said. The location is great and later on you could develop it into a restaurant.

Ronnie buckled, his jaw falling to the floor. Joyce backed away a couple of steps. The kitchen got hot from body temperatures rising. Ronnie was stunned. Joyce seemed aloof. I looked at dad and his narrow Clark Gable mustache rose higher on his lip.

This is an opportunity of a lifetime, dad said. You can own your own business, manage it, work there, be creative and make money.

You're giving the Doggie Diner to us, Ronnie said.

We'll discuss details of ownership exchange later.

I don't want the Diner, Ronnie said. I'm studying cultural anthropology at City College. That takes up all my time.

What about you, Joyce, dad said. You want the Doggie Diner, don't you?

She shook her head. I don't want the Diner either. I have a job at the bank.

The Doggie Diner is yours. Both of you can manage it. You can have your own business and you're barely twenty-one years old. Opportunity is knocking at your doors. What else would you do with your lives?

I don't want it. Ronnie's voice filled with irritation and he turned to leave the kitchen. I'll soon be headed to the University in Mexico City.

Owning your own business is better than going to college, dad said. Better yet, you can own your own business and go to college at the same time.

Mom was busy listening and slicing up the roast in its pan on the opened oven door. The roasting fragrance of meat, onions, carrots and potatoes filled the house.

Static drifted around the kitchen. The electric clock on the shelf beside the kitchen nook emitted a low buzz. The Admiral

Refrigerator motor kicked on. Missy came out of nowhere and stood sniffing and watching mom slice the roast.

The body language between my two older siblings radiated many effects; exasperation, anger, resentment, annoyance and distrust were just a few of those effects. Ronnie and Joyce stood in place as frozen statues.

Dad's breathing was shallow, his posture stiff and his demeanor expressed finality. Okay, he said. Neither of you want the Doggie Diner. Don't ever tell me that I'd never tried to give you anything.

That was the end of the Doggie Diner and the end of dad's fatherly relationship with Ronnie and Joyce. His offer and their rejections, that's what family life was like as I'd watched my brother and sister, fade into the background. That was also the beginning of our Sunday dinner of which I'd enjoyed, of which Ronnie and Joyce didn't partake.

After that encounter, dad seldom hung-out with any of us, and when we did get the chance to be with him, he was preoccupied with ideas and inventions; drawing and designing gadgets like a mini-fire extinguisher and Adirondack style lawn furniture. He was the inventor and I was his ignored puppet wanting attention, except that he never pulled my strings so I could come to life.

His questionable friends were few like Jackson, the black mechanic that helped dad work on his cars on the upside dirt driveway. Jackson never came inside the house, he worked on the cars and sweated and that was that. The Edward G. Robinson look-a-like business partner with dad, usually wore a dark suit, hung his thumbs off his vest and always had a cigar either between his fingers or lips. He was a strange character to me, hanging around in the background, observing, maybe filled with a type of care-free charm with complicated thoughts, ideas he couldn't express, and fleeting emotions that went unsaid. I projected my thoughts about him onto myself. I didn't understand how much of a business partner Mr. Cooper and dad were, just that they entertained, consulted and demonstrated dad's inventions together at the house to would-be manufactures and buyers.

On special days with cooking homemade French fries for

lunch with Karen, playing with Ronnie's knife in the empty lot across the street and roller-skating with Karen on the Monroe Elementary School playground, we'd had a full day of fun. With mom sweating in the kitchen baking pot roast for dinner, then after dinner, retiring to a dimly lit living room watching several Sunday programs on television, the family gatherings seemed monumental.

    We'd watch the Jack Benny Program then switch the channel to Mr. Peepers or to the Ed Sullivan Show, sometimes even the Loretta Young show was interesting on our seventeen-inch Admiral Television. Timmy and Karen would sit on the cracked leather sofa with dad. Mom would be sitting on her wheelchair beside me. I'd be on my knees by the living room window and stare at the towering illuminated cross on Mt. Davidson miles away across the valley, wondering if Jesus was crucified on such a monstrous beautiful cross.

Personal Context

STOPPING SPONTANEOUS events from happening during my childhood was impossible. Recalling the unplanned or impulsive events was also impossible. The events I recall are the ones most important, the ones that shaped my personality, the ones that won't vacate my memory, the ones that haunted me for a few years afterward, the ones that my siblings and friends wouldn't let me forget, the ones that drove me crazy if I'd let them, the ones that were so ridiculous, dreadful, awkward, irresolvable, yet unavoidable and yet so hopeless that they would become my mini-bible of what not to say and do to others. Well, most of the few events I recall weren't insufferably bad, but they were as I said, awkward.

When mom spoke to me her words may have sounded poetic, but they formed sentences that made statements or commands. Dad seldom spoke to me and when he did his guidance didn't make me intelligent, yet they made common sense. When Timmy, Karen and I played, our communications consisted of running, jumping, yelling, pushing, tickling and punching, standing in silence, making faces and sometimes watching out for each other.

For all that mattered to me when I was ten years old I'd known that I'd have to be braver than my emotions.

Our last summer we'd spent at our shack in Oroville in 1955, I was burned out on everything; the distressing heat, chores of cleaning the outhouse, retrieving jugs of water from the bar/restaurant down the road, swatting at mosquitos, killing insufferable flies landing on our food and faces, pushing mom in her wheelchair down the dirt pathway a hundred feet from the house to the car and back when we'd return, bathing in the creek and even swimming in Feather River was a chore. We could pick so many blackberries and strawberries to eat, ride our bicycles a half-mile before heat exhaustion settled in, swim in the mosquito infested water hole without drowning, and the last two events were so devastating I'd never want to return to

Oroville again.

The first event was during one special night when Missy went missing. She was a member of the family and slept inside the shack with the rest of us. She was always at our feet wanting in on any action we could muster. She would whimper when she wanted out of the house, she would growl when agitated, she would sneeze and grin when she was happy to see us, she would bump into our legs and walk around us when she wanted attention, like a bath or brushing. Missy was our mascot and she went missing.

The next morning, Missy came to the front door of the shack and scratched on the screen door to get in. We let her in. her jowls were filled with porcupine barbs, long and needle like, at least twenty of them scattered around her lower jaw and up along her whiskers. The rest of the day was filled with dad and Ronnie and a neighbor holding Missy down against her will, twisting and angling and pulling the barbs out of her face. The inside tips of the barbs were hooked, designed for not coming out of its victim. Missy was that porcupine's sad victim.

For at least two hours Missy yelped, growled and kicked to get away from the people that pained her face. They tried tying her legs together and that didn't work. None of them were strong enough to steady her. Two held her down and one-by-one our neighbor twisted the barbs out of her face with pliers. Missy was devastated and I cried over her suffering.

Timmy mowing tall grass in Oroville

The second event was the forest fire burning ancient oak trees and thick four-foot-tall dried grass across the acreage beside our shack. During summers the whole Oroville countryside was a probable incendiary landscape, the excessive heat nonetheless acting as the eventual spark to blazing catastrophes.

The fire looked so far away, yet the flames combusted into an incandescent inferno that threatened our shack twenty feet from the ten-foot-tall flames. The fire devoured the dry acreage west of our house was one hundred percent out of control.

Every summer, after we'd arrive at our shack we'd retrieve dad's electric lawnmower from the house and cut down all the waist-high dead yellow weeds from around our entire property, making the dry ground a play land for insects, snakes, gophers, raccoons, deer, bobcats and an occasional mountain lion. If we hadn't done that our shack along with our emotions would have been ashes saturating the ground.

We couldn't do anything to fight the fire. Our well was dry so we had to extinguish small cinders near our shack with a couple of rakes and shovels. The county fire department did their job, containing and drowning the blaze that same day. The odor of ashes lingered in our clothes and property and the taste of burnt grass and debris loitered in our mouths for the rest of our stay that summer at the shack.

WITH ONE week left to stay at the end of the summer of 1955 in Oroville, Karen and I were discouraged with the whole Oroville crap-shoot. We wanted to go home to San Francisco, have the cool, misty fog swirl around our bodies while playing outside, go to Playland and eat corndogs and pink cotton candy and most of all we craved the fragrance of the crisp Pacific Ocean air. That wouldn't happen for another week, so while we waited we'd stage games like fist-fights.

One fight started innocently. We'd stood face to face, Karen's grim mug, squinty eyes and downturned mouth was six inches above my angered confrontation. You have to remember that I was ten and Karen was twelve years old. She was heavyset and weighed maybe twenty pounds more than me. She was as intimidating to me as a heavyweight boxer to a welterweight puppy, but to each other, this playful act was as menacing as a brother and sister could get.

We stood under the large oak tree on the dirt driveway fifty feet from the shack. Taking turns pulling our right arms back, we'd make fists and fake punch each other in the face. On my forth punch my tight fist in a roundhouse punch accidentally whacked Karen upside her head and she went down hard on the dirt.

I panicked and screamed and stooped down, Karen squirmed, shook her head and jumped up. I jumped up with her.

Dirty little fucker, she said.

I ran around the tree. In chase she followed. I stammered and faked turns, keeping the large oak tree trunk between us.

I'm going to kill you, she yelled. You slugged me and I'm going to kill you.

I ran up the pathway to the house. Mom was in her wheelchair sunbathing and reading a paperback book beside a lawn chair. Ronnie came running out of the house.

Karen ran after me. I sprinted around the backside of the house. She followed at a distance so as not to fall on the fire ashes. After running scared around the rest of the shack to the front and back to the old tree, Ronnie scampered up the path and stood between Karen and me.

She called me a fucker and said she's going to kill me, I yelled at Ronnie while Karen reached around him grabbing at me.

You called Benny a fucker, Ronnie pushed at Karen.

I'm going to kill him for punching me in the face, Karen said.

Accidents happen, I yelled. Then I climbed up the old oak tree out of reach from both of them. I knew that either Ronnie or Karen was going to kill me before we went back to 402 Avalon.

Stay in the tree until you cool off, Ronnie said, spying up at me and tightly gripping Karen by the shoulder. If I see either of you fighting again, I'll beat both of you up.

That's not fair, Karen yelled. He punched me in the face and I get to punch him in the face.

Get down here, Benny, and let Karen punch you in the

face. Ronnie's anger scared me.

I descended, straightened my shorts and stood in front of Karen. My nervous face was six inches below her bullying face. Ronnie stood back. Karen made a fist, swung her arm around and stopped the frightening, devastating punch in front of my nose. She giggled and pushed me down on my butt. The worst thing about our fake fight was the dozens of weed stickers that punctured my butt when I fell. I had to pull them out and bleed over the next few minutes. Karen's inner sinister-self knew that would happen, terrorizing me without punching me in the face.

BACK IN San Francisco after our last summer in Oroville during 1955, I'd settled in with my spontaneous antics that were contrite, and as I said, awkward. Summer was over, sixth grade would start the first week of September and a bunch of hoopla in my family was about to happen.

At my young age most events that occurred in the family was surprising to me. During the last two years I'd seen a few science fiction and horror movies at the Granada Theater that were surprising and scary, movies like *Bride of the Monster* and The *Quatermass Xperiment*, but I knew they weren't real and they didn't shape my young outlook about life, but they weren't as surprising as the events in my family.

Many small and large incidents I'd experienced however enjoyable or distressing they were, shaped my outlook about life for my future. One such event started when Timmy and Karen locked me out of the house. Oh yeah, I'd already told you about that, and the long-jagged scar down the ulnar side of my right palm still proves that I'd punched the window out. I like my beautiful scar now.

One cool afternoon Timmy and I were bragging to Bobby Eliot about the two of us throwing our opponents one-by-one over our backs in Judo classes. Ronnie had us take Judo classes with him every Friday night. One Saturday afternoon Timmy and I stood with Bobby on the sidewalk corner of Avalon Avenue and Madrid Street above the empty lot.

Prove to me how you threw someone over your shoulder,

Bobby said to Timmy. Show me how you throw somebody over your back.

Timmy twisted his hips, grabbed Bobby by his shoulder sleeves, lifted his leg upward to unsettle Bobby's legs and flung Bobby over his back. The problem was that Timmy held onto Bobby's shoulders for a controlled flip. Bobby's hard shoes landed on the concrete, one heel struck full-force on my left foot. My leather shoes were old and soft and I yanked my left foot to my waist and yelped aye-ya aye-ya aye-ya aye-ya aye. After checking that I was fine Timmy and Bobby laughed at me. As I cried and left the scene, hopping across the cross-walk I yelled over my shoulder that I was going to tell mom. But I didn't. To this day, whenever I hear someone say aye-ya aye-ya aye-ya-aye-ya, I fly back to 1956.

Benny & Timmy in traditional Judogi 1955

After a picnic during Saturday at Memorial Park with the Webb family, we gathered in the kitchen at home. Mom was bent over sitting on her wheelchair shedding her dirty shoes. I put my hand on her back. One of the few times I'd touched mom and wouldn't you know it, a bee stung my palm. That felt like a surprise handshake buzzer but the stinger kept stinging. I pulled my hand away, the bee dropped to the floor and I yelped. Mom dropped her dirty shoe on the clean floor and everybody laughed at me. I dug at my palm for three minutes with a needle and tweezers to get the stinger out of the center of my hand. I don't have a scar to prove what happened, but I have the memory of everybody laughing at me. Ha, ha, ha.

Mom's favorite two girlfriends were Ann Cram and Bertha Webb. Mom told me that they'd met each other when all our families lived in the Projects while their husbands were employed by Bethlehem Steel. They continued their friendship after we'd moved to the Gerard Street house and then moved into 402 Avalon.

Ann Cram was roly-poly; a short and plump lady, with a hearty laugh and a good spirit, always with a brown Perm hairdo. I looked upon her as a comic strip character in the Sunday Examiner. Ann with her husband Joe owned a large piece of property in Oroville that was cleared of oak trees. They'd vacationed there, staying in their Airstream Clipper trailer. The trailer was recognizable by the distinctive shape of their rounded aluminum bodies. Whenever the Cram's came to Oroville during the summers we'd visit them, but I'd avoided stepping up into their Airstream Clipper. To me the trailer looked like a small helium Blimp that would explode any second.

Bertha Webb was tall and plump. Her straight black hair revealed her American Indian heritage. She was serious with a wry sense of humor. I'd always looked at mom and her friends as elderly when in fact all three were about forty years old. Cram and Webb were constants on Thursday or Friday nights at our house during the early 1950s, always playing cards. Three-in-one rummy was their favorite card game, but when one of them came over they would play Gin Rummy. When they played cards they always ordered Chinese food delivery. Mom would let me stay up late so when the food arrived she'd serve me up a plate of delicious beef Chow Mein, fried rice and two Fortune Cookies.

Mrs. Bertha Webb came over one Saturday night dragging

her son Gordon with her. Gordon and I were the same age and height, but he was a little chubby and I was thin. Mrs. Webb and mom were going to play cards and Gordon and I were to play something of our choice. Since Gordon was half Nez Perce Indian on his mother's side and half Caucasian on his father's side, I'd decided Gordon and I should play cowboys and Indians. After all I had the hat, boots, toy six-shooters and one bow and arrow and a headdress for him. In my small bedroom dressing up I'd handed Gordon the bow and arrow. He put them on the bed. I handed him the feather headdress. He handed the headband back to me.

I don't want to be the Indian, he said. You're Tonto and I'm the Lone Ranger.

You can't be the Lone Ranger, I said. He's white and you're a real Indian.

I know I'm a real Indian, he said. But Indians are cowboys, too. You're Tonto and I'm the Lone Ranger.

Pulling my chaps off from over my pants, boots, six-shooter holsters and hat, I shook my head sideways and handed each one of them to Gordon and watched him dress up. He looked like an Indian cowboy. I put the feather headdress on and a small vest over my white t-shirt, my slippers acted as moccasins, I then picked up the bow and arrow and charged into the kitchen with Gordon on my heels. Mrs. Webb and mom were in the middle of a Rummy hand. They looked our way and started laughing. We laughed with them. Gordon and I played cowboy and Indian for another two hours, exhaustion taking us to the living room to watch an old Roy Rogers and Gabby Hayes western movie. After that night I'd never played cowboys and Indians again thanks to Gordon Webb.

On Sunday February 5, 1956, I recall the date because that day was a turning point in my life. For some forgotten reason Timmy and Bobby Harnwell teased me that afternoon. They ran inside Bobby's backyard and closed the gate to the tall fence and wouldn't let me in. I stood on our property across the street in our upside dirt driveway. I felt strong and delirious. They bobbed their heads up and down behind the fence, the style of now you see me now you don't.

After picking up a rock the size of a golf ball, feeling the weight and size in my hand, a blaze of cruelty overcame me. My head burned with anger and I hissed through my teeth. I tossed the rock at my enemies, hitting the fence just below Timmy's station behind the fence.

Their heads continued to bob. Their antagonizing statements and laughter incensed me beyond belief. I picked up another rock which was as large as the first one. Their heads bobbed, I tossed the fucking rock with all my strength and bang. The rock hit Bobby Harnwell on the forehead between his eyes and he fell. In shock I ran from the driveway and stood in the middle of Avalon Avenue.

Silence filled the air. I killed my best friend, I'd hit him in the head with a heavy rock and killed the friend that was always filled with fun and laughter when we'd go horseback riding, swimming at the YMCA, riding busses to Playland, my friend I took to my dad's employer Christmas party where he'd won the grand prize, the boy whose parents drove us up to Clear Lake and we'd rowed a small boat all afternoon, my neighbor who was going to be my best friend for the rest of my life.

I'd killed Bobby Harnwell.

Not really.

Bobby's head was suddenly above the fence ascending the six stairs to the small backdoor deck. Then his shoulders appeared. One hand covered his forehead while he opened the door to his house. He looked at me standing in the middle of the street, nodded and went inside. Not killing Bobby was the best thing I'd done in my life up to that time.

My moment of discovery was that I'd have to be braver than my emotions. Instead of crying about the atrocity I'd done to my best friend, I laughed. My sense of humor was replicating Karen's more and more every day.

During next Sunday's family dinner, sitting at the kitchen nook, dad started choking. He jumped up out of the nook, bend over and tried to gulp air but now came. Ronnie jumped up and pounded on dad's back. Mom tried to give him a glass of water. He pushed Ronnie away and stalled mom with hand gestures. He rose up with his arms overhead like Moses parting the Red Sea. His face turned red and he doubled over. I jumped out of the nook, ran through the kitchen, down the long hallway and out the front door.

Jesus, you can't let dad die, I said, while kneeling down on the porch. If this is the only time I ask something from you then you have to help. Don't let dad die, he's too young to die.

I waited and prayed. I'd said the Lord's Prayer many times at bedtime but I'd never faced the subject of death in our home. 402 Avalon, was this our home or our death trap.

Warm arms encircled my shoulders and picked me up off my knees. Joyce came to my rescue. Dad's fine, she said. You know how dad doesn't like to eat meat. A small chicken bone got lodged in his neck and he pulled it out. He's fine, come inside and finish your diner.

My prayer was answered.

RONNIE'S OCTOBER birthday came and went unnoticed in 1955 by family members except for mom. Ronnie was her favorite child. He had turned twenty-one, and the time had arrived for him to leave the country, go to Mexico and attend the University, just get out of my hair. Thank goodness.

Thanksgiving Day came and went unnoticed, except by me. Ronnie hadn't left for Mexico yet. So, what he did for our Thanksgiving dinner was kill my pet turkey Clarabell. I named my turkey after Clarabell the clown on the Howdy Doody television show. The last four letters of his name were the last four letters of my last name.

My older brother Ronnie pushed me through the house to the backyard and made me watch while he held Clarabell's legs together. With wings flapping Ronnie positioned him sideways on a short tree stump, lifted a large axe off the ground and chopped off Clarabell's head.

With eyes wide open, Clarabell's beak was askew with his tongue hanging out. The finger that sits atop his face between the beak and the eyes flopped down. His head flopped off the side of the tree stump, his red wattle flipped sideways as his head plopped on the dirt beside my feet.

My pet turkey snapped his legs out of Ronnie's grip. Headless Clarabell stood up and took off running across the yard like Wile E. Coyote, wings flapping, tail flaring, and his head across the yard remained dead beside my feet. Blood spurted everywhere from Clarabell's neck like a geyser. He ran, tripped and fell, stood up and ran some more.

Tears cut paths down my cheeks as I watched Clarabell. Anxiety moans escaped between my lips that could be heard a block away.

Clarabell stumbled, trying to stay alive, tripping on small dirt piles, slamming into the fence then falling on his side. His feet twitched. A rustling silence filled my heart.

Ronnie watched the race of death with a knowing smile. What better lesson for you to learn, Benny, Ronnie said, dying is part of living and you have to face the fact that all things die. We eat turkey on Thanksgiving Day and tonight we'll eat Clarabell.

I didn't eat turkey that Thanksgiving. I didn't eat anything.

Clarabell was dead and Ronnie killed him. The rest of my family ate Clarabell and didn't seem concerned that he was my pet. Clarabell's blood stains on the dirt would erode and be absorbed, but the stains on the back wooden fence would remain.

Aside from getting booted out of the Monroe School Glee Club, Thursday November 24, 1955, Thanksgiving Day, was the worst day of my life. Ronnie had to get out of the house and go to Mexico.

The second worst day in my life was my attempted kidnapping the day before Halloween. The evening's overcast sky was eerie enough let alone having to walk home three blocks from Yvonne's house in the dark deserted streets of the Excelsior District.

Yvonne was my good friend and confident in the sixth grade at school. Her parents wouldn't let her go outside at dusk. At least once a week I'd stand on the sidewalk outside her bedroom window at 204 Paris Street and she'd hang out the window and face me. We had a connection because her address of 204 was the reverse of my address. As ten-year old's we'd confide with each other about school subjects and personal matters like flying kites in the empty lot and how far we could throw rocks.

When I started walking home at six thirty, a 1950 black Chevrolet started following me when I'd turned the corner from Paris to Excelsior Streets. Three city blocks up the grade and I'd be home.

Not so fast.

I walked slowly and the car drove slower and stayed behind me. I walked faster and the car stayed on my heels. If I was educated about the dangers of strangers and deserted streets, then I would have been prepared. But I wasn't educated and I wasn't prepared. I was just a scared boy wanting to get home after a fun time chatting with Yvonne.

My heart pounded, I sweated and fear controlled me. The air was cold and I was overheated. I walked one block up on Excelsior Street and crossed the intersection at Lisbon Street. The car was behind me and driving fast.

I panicked and ran down Lisbon, passed Monroe School, turned right into the bottom of the steep empty lot. The car jumped the curb and started driving over the tall weeds that was indigenous to the lot. I panicked again and changed course, fell on my hip and slid down thirty feet on the slick wet weeds back to the sidewalk. The car backed up. I ran back down Excelsior to Lisbon, across the crosswalk and jumped up the dozen stairs on the second house from the corner.

Like a maniac I pounded my fists on the front door. Nobody answered. I'd hoped the driver of the car believed that this house was my home. A light came on in the front window, the curtain pushed aside but nobody was there.

An Italian looking woman, the likes of a frumpy Gina Lollobrigida no taller than me answered the door. She looked me up and down like I was a piece of meat.

What do you want?

I cried. There's a car chasing me and I'm scared.

Go home, she said and slammed the door on me.

I turned around and faced the street. The black car was driving down the hill in the opposite direction. I jumped down the stairs to the sidewalk and ran like a cheetah all the way home, almost throwing up from exhaustion at my front door, wanting to rest in my small room that I had to share with Ronnie.

The front door to our house was locked. Without my key, I pounded on the door. Ronnie opened it and vice-gripped my arm. I was out of breath and sweating like a waterfall. He pushed me against the opened door.

What happened to you?

A car chased me and I was running to escape it, I said.

Stop lying, he said. I won't let you in the house until you tell me from where you stole those coins?

Missy came to my rescue. She butted between Ronnie and me, wagging her tail and sneezing a greeting. I sat down on the front door threshold and hugged my favorite family member. She never complained or questioned me. She just licked my face, wagged her tail, nudged my hands and whimpered. That night I'd taken a hot bath and wondered just what people were all about. They weren't friendly to me and who knew what devious agendas they believed in.

My comfort over the next month before Christmas was watching older western movies on television on Saturday and Sunday mornings; movies that starred the whip-carrying, tough-talking Lash LaRue, the subtle soft-talking singing cowboy Gene Autry, "King of the Cowboys" Roy Rogers and the side-swaggering John Wayne among a few others like the Lone Ranger and Hopalong Cassidy. During weekdays I rushed home to watch *Howdy Doody* on television among other late afternoon shows before dinner. My life was still incomplete without Clarabell, but for one exception, another animal was in my life and helping me cope with my loss and she was Missy.

Anticipating Christmas was a godsend. The holiday took my thoughts off the murder of Clarabell by my insensitive brother. Christmas was all I'd thought about; shopping for the perfect tree with mom, setting up the tree and decorating the branches, purchasing the coffee warmer as my gift to mom, wrapping the delicate present and setting my gift to mom under the tree was the best feeling.

Karen and Timmy kidded me the entire month of December about the coffee warmer. In the presence of our mom they would mumble cooffeewwaarrmmeerr. Red-faced with anger I felt abused and hammered over the teasing. But I could withstand the bantering and mocking because I was Snap,

Crackle or Pop, one of the loving Rice Krispies Kids.

I didn't want mom to know about my gift and she pretended that she didn't know. She'd snicker and look away whenever Timmy and Karen said cooffeewwaarrmmeerr. I was comforted about her not knowing, but deep inside I knew she knew and hated knowing that.

Each day one week before Christmas I'd waited for presents to appear underneath the tree. When presents suddenly appeared I'd read the name tags. All the presents were for my sisters, brothers, mom and dad and none for me. Not one gift under the tree was for me until Christmas morning. I knew Santa was fiction, why couldn't I get gifts under the tree before Christmas like other family members? I felt left out, the forgotten kid, the last child in the family that nobody cared about. In truth, my heart was broken that Christmas. I wanted to recapture my innocence, my boyishness, any happiness I could muster and most of all, the laughter I'd felt inside, yet all of that had vanished by way of incivility.

Life wasn't all that bad. At least I had love from my pet dog Missy, and how great was that, a dog and a boy all alone at 402 Avalon Avenue.

Missy Greeting Me

BEGINNING WITH my eleventh birthday on January 17, 1956, I had a core feeling that living at 402 Avalon was either a huge mistake by my parents or the house offered huge benefits. I'd believed that my family members throughout the past five years were learning from their mistakes, or that they were at least learning not to make mistakes concerning their lives.

On a Tuesday morning I'd awakened to whispers in my ear but nothing was there. A few minutes later I jerked to a sitting position in bed from a distant scream, a woman in distress maybe. Did mom scream? I listened for another scream but none happened. I locked my eyes on Ronnie's white glowing wind-up clock sitting on top of the dresser. Ronnie was snoring and the time was 3 am.

I edged off the upper bunk to the floor, stumbled through the kitchen, the hallway and in to the bathroom to take a leak. If only some noise like creaking from the house would happen, but this time the silence killed me.

I closed the door and in the dark, I sat down on the toilet seat. What was that whispering and where did that scream come from? Chills crisscrossed my little body. I looked to my right and someone was lying motionless in the bathtub. Darkness hampered my vision. Someone else was in front of me standing beside the sink. They were adults. The woman in the tub had death written all over her naked body. The bearded disheveled man at the sink held a straight shaving razor. I blinked and held my breath then put my hands over my face and peed.

Nobody is there, I murmured. Nothing is wrong. With eyes closed I ignored my guests and understood that the whispering and the scream came from this bathroom. I stood up, flushed the toilet, whisked across the kitchen and went back to bed, lying awake until 7 am when I got up to get ready for school.

That entire day I was outside my body, observing myself from a distance like an invisible ghost, scrutinizing every exchange I'd had with friends at school and each new thought I'd proposed to myself. My home, the old Brown Farm that was built sometime during the 1880s was alive and well, scrutinizing every person living within its walls throughout the decades, squeezing and pampering its history through periods of upgrades and changes of the guard. Something had to be done about past dead lives coming back to life within my home.

People and issues disturbed me and that included my

family and 402 Avalon. The alarming factors were the complications my family and the house created for all of us.

My anxiety flipped into frustration about my teachers in school and some sort-of obstruction of my interests from family members. The way they conversed in clichés and the commands they conjured up like, *don't walk like a duck, don't go to bed in your underpants, don't dirty your clothes when playing outside.*

I'd resisted attempts from Ronnie and mom of making me conform to their rules of behavior, how they thought I should act and interact with people. Disobeying and willful defiance weren't issues with me. Realizing I'd felt isolated in school and at home was extraordinary. The feeling was less hubris and meeker, and I had to find an outlet or ways of avoiding family demanding that I follow their social lead; saying what they said and doing what they did, like a clone or robot without a mind of my own.

Learning what was morally and ethically acceptable wasn't a problem either, I just wanted to greet people my way, to say hi and ask questions about them. Mom and Ronnie disciplined me, telling me not to speak unless spoken to, not to say anything and stay in the background. My social relationship with the world was to shut up and become invisible to everybody.

I'd not thought about the chores I had to perform, but when I was eleven years old one main chore maddened me once a month. Mom would give me a handful of dollar bills with a note to take to Julianni's. The neighborhood store was a small house converted to a grocery store around the block on Excelsior Avenue.

Behind the cash register counter Julianni, with her Italian accent would read the note aloud that mom gave me, grab a long rod, walk to the front of the store, pull two large packages off the top shelf over the front door and have me stand there and catch them in my arms. Customers would watch and I'd be embarrassed. Tampax packages, they were large and cumbersome and I'd have to carry them in plain sight back home around the block. Just why I was given the chore of purchasing mom and Joyce's personal hygiene product once a month was beyond me.

Julianni's was my favorite place. Beside the cash register

was an enclosed glass meat display. Since my treasury discovery in the garage I always had money. Saturdays I'd sneak out of the house and head for Julianni's. For twenty-five cents she'd slice up salami and Swiss cheese on the electric slicer and make a large sandwich on a sourdough French roll with plenty of mustard. In the sixth grade on Wednesdays I'd go purchase a salami sandwich and sit with a satisfied smile on my face in class for the rest of the school afternoon.

School was tedious and torturous and tasteless during my younger grades. My family ignored me and any progress I'd made learning to read and write seemed worthless. The world of reading and writing was one of right and wrong and black and white, and within that framework I was clueless about everything. The homonyms and groups of words that share the same spelling and the same pronunciation confused me. Too many words like bow and bough that are spelled differently and pronounced the same and have different meanings, I couldn't make sense (cents) of the English language.

Sixth grade was exceptional for me. My teacher Miss Hunt was an attractive young woman. She helped me memorize all the presidents of the United States and understand the three branches of federal government. Her artistic mind instructed me how to draw human figures and use colors to describe emotional moods.

Other than reading, writing and arithmetic and history lessons during school days, after art class and two recesses I was exhausted. During the year holiday celebrations and field trips exhausted me more, but the glee club was my savior. I was a member of the glee club and I was also a street crossing-guard. Becoming a street-guard was a grounding responsibility. Our 1956 crossing-guard march at Kezar Stadium, located adjacent to Kezar Pavilion in the southeastern corner of Golden Gate Park in San Francisco, was the most fun in sixth grade as a communal event.

I loved being a member of the glee club more than being a crossing-guard, helping silly kids cross the street. They knew to look left and right, the drivers of cars didn't seem to know when or where to stop to let the kids cross in front of them, but nobody was run over or killed on my watch.

As a glee club member, twice a week Miss Hunt excused me from my regular class for one hour, and I assembled with the other twenty glee-club members in the largest classroom on the second floor of Monroe School. On an impromptu stage, we sang older and popular songs. The gathering of students, to me, was more social than educational. The blending of various voices of twenty kids was frustrating, and during uncommon moments our harmonies were alluring, meaning we looked stunned and couldn't believe our voices could sound pleasant, like a bunch of ducks quacking on the bank of Stow Lake in Golden Gate Park.

All of that was great until rehearsal one Thursday afternoon when Mr. Howard, our glee club instructor, kicked me out of the club. I stumbled on the words to the song *She'll Be Coming Around the Mountain*. He waved his hand overhead, meaning for all of us to shut up. He pointed at me and put a finger over his lips to hush the mumbling. He slithered all over like a snake and he asked me, why didn't you learn the lyrics? You had since Tuesday to learn the lyrics. Learning the lyrics is mandatory.

I was a quiet kid and now I was embarrassed. I memorized all the presidents of the United States, including the names of each state, I said. I did that to pass a test we had this morning in Miss Hunt's class.

That's not relevant, he said. You have to memorize all the words to the song to stay in my glee club.

I'm sorry, I said. Miss Hunt said if we made a mistake we would have to take the test over. I wanted to answer every question correctly.

That's your problem not my glee club's problem.

I'm sorry, I said a second time. I'll learn the lyrics.

Don't bother learning the lyrics, Benny Campbell, he said. As of right now you're expelled from my glee club. Pack up and go back to Miss Hunt's class.

Can I stay, Mr. Howard? I've been in the club for eight weeks. I like to sing and you said I have a good voice.

I can't make an exception, he said, and pointed at the door. When you don't learn the lyrics, you can't stay in my glee club.

All eyes were glued on me. I stepped down off the top tier

of the stage, grabbed my jacket off the back of a chair and dashed to the door. Tears welled up. I glanced at the club members and all their eyes were affixed on Mr. Howard. He hit his conductor stick on the desk and raised both arms overhead. Without looking at me, in a stern voice he said, please close the door behind you.

For the love of all that was holy, my life was instantly crushed. I felt like an angel whose wings were hacked off for no reason. Evicted from the Monroe School glee club was humiliating. I would be teased by classmates, mocked with failure because I couldn't even memorize words to a simple song. I wiped tears away with my shirt sleeve and staggered down the long hallway back to Miss Hunt's class. All my classmates were inside reading about Abraham Lincoln, and I was the least emancipated. I leaned against the hallway wall beside the door and cried.

If only my name wasn't Albert Benjamin Campbell. My initials ABC stood for *always-being-criticized*. And then, I'd recalled watching on television the comedy, *Your Show of Shows*, starring Sid Caesar and Imogene Coca. I'd watched that show a few Saturday evenings with my family, yet I didn't understand much of the social implications until that moment sitting on the floor crying like a baby. Everything that had happened to me was actually funny and not tragic. I would get over being kicked out of the glee club and I'd just have to sing by myself.

Over the next few weekends comedy TV shows I'd watch were *The Red Skelton Hour, I Love Lucy, The Jack Benny Program, The Abbot and Costello Show, The Little Rascals, The Honeymooners, The Phil Silvers Show, The Bob Cummings Show, The George Burns and Gracie Allen Show, The Life of Riley,* and a few others that had less social impact nevertheless were funny.

Most of the comedy TV shows were stylishly creative and underpinned with cultural impingements and comedic skits. They had subliminal sexual nuances, revealing gender inequalities with hints of political incorrectness. Dad would sometimes watch such TV shows with us on weekend nights. We'd gather in the living room, me beside the window so I could look across the valley and see the cross under lit on top of Mt. Davidson. Surprising was the fact that dad liked watching and listening to the Liberace Show. He enjoyed watching most of the comedy shows and that included the Amos and Andy show.

Dad had an ear for music and that seemed logical since mom played the piano and accordion. He also had a need to laugh and the comedy television shows afforded him that pleasure. Dad was a music aficionado and the few times I'd heard him sing a few lyrics he sounded like Nat King Cole. He was also a laughter fiend. I would never have known that if we didn't go see *Francis the Talking Mule* movies.

However, behind the scenes of music and comedy and family dinners and outings, frustrations were constant curtains that needed to be opened. I wasn't privy to many family conversations and arguments, yet I knew that they were ongoing behind closed doors and in small groups consisting of just mom and dad, or mom and dad with Ronnie, or mom and dad with Joyce.

One unraveling, argumentative occurrence captured my undivided attention. Dad called a family meeting in the kitchen. Timmy, Karen and I sat in the nook dad had built into the wall. Mom sat in her wheelchair. She wanted me out of the earshot. Dad refused and told her that I was old enough to understand. Ronnie stood to the side.

Dad confronted Joyce.

What I recall about dad's declaration is explicit, but the conversation that ensued is all a blur. Joyce had to marry the younger man she'd fallen head-over-heels for. Dad's serious demeanor could cut a diamond. He didn't like the kid. He didn't like the kid's mother. As for the kid's father, where the hell was he not helping to raise the Catholic kid.

Entrusting your love with a younger man is disgraceful, dad said. Staying out all night and coming home at odd hours of the morning is more than disgraceful, it's dishonorable and deceitful. You're pregnant. Here's one hundred dollars, go to Reno and get married.

He handed her the money. Don't come back to this house, I never want to see you again.

That was the end of her filial piety in our American Nuclear family.

The family meeting ended. All of us scattered to our rooms. I jumped up on the top of my bunk bed, put my face in my pillow and cried for a while. When I turned over, put my hands behind my head and stared at the ceiling I'd thought, maybe I'd lived at 402 Avalon too long.

That was the beginning of the end of our family and I was eleven years old. Ronnie was going to the University of Mexico in Mexico City. Joyce was excommunicated from the family. Mom was planning a driving trip across the States during the summer of 1956 to visit her dad and brothers in Butler, Pennsylvania in which Timmy, Karen and I would go with her. After dad's declaration to Joyce, I wandered what would happen between mom and dad, worse yet, what would happen to all of us.

The next morning, I woke up to find that my large glass piggy bank that I'd hid in the corner of the room was broken and empty. I had thirty dollars in coins and paper bills saved inside of it. Joyce was gone, so was her suitcase and clothes, so was my money and so was her past as a member of the Campbell family. That may have been the end of Joyce in the Campbell family, but that wasn't her end. Her life was just beginning and mom would help her along the way by getting and paying for her new apartment before we left on our motor trip back east.

My ears listened and my eyes watched the events taking place. My past was over and my future was now. The San Francisco I'd loved was a fluid city that was always changing with progressive social issues.

If I laughed, wouldn't everything be alright?

Truths & Lies

FALLACIES, DECEPTIONS, truths and lies, reality and fiction are what novels are made of, and all of that had also applied to members of the young Campbell family. I didn't know which truths were lies or which lies were truths, all I knew was that stories were told by mom and dad, narratives were exchanged and statements were just statements. Whether the stories were fairytales, inventions, fabrications or even excuses, many family issues weren't resolved in my young inquisitive mind.

Mom told me that dad was adopted from a family in Texas and taken to live in Pennsylvania. That dad's read name was Claude Holmes of German descent and that he had a twin brother that was adopted and taken to live in Canada. Joyce told me that dad's real last name was spelled as Holems, and not Holmes. What was I to believe?

Mom showed me a clipping from a Canadian newspaper. The story was about a celebrated fly-fisherman who had won a Canadian fishing contest and the accompanying photo was a clone of dad. Our father didn't travel to Canada, he'd never fished and he wasn't one for gathering attention. Whether he had a twin or was even adopted was an issue for me. Was Claude Holems dad's real name? Was my last name Holems, or Holmes, or was it Campbell?

Tim and I visited dad together in 1995 and I'd asked about his adoption. He said he could remember back to when he was about three years old, that he had traveled and lived in another state and had different parents. All of that to me was circumstantial and not confirmation that he was adopted. Truth or lie I'd never find out.

I don't recall who told me this, but mom was allegedly raped by her cousin just after she and dad were married. She'd become pregnant and gave birth to Ronnie, her first child. Thus, Ronnie was our half-brother. During family gatherings for Sunday dinner's dad appeared aloof to Ronnie.

From what I recall, dad and Ronnie argued about topics

such as philosophy, anthropology and the self-defense Judo club that Ronnie had joined and recruited Timmy and me to join.

What good is Judo, dad said to Ronnie, when the guy you're fighting is stronger than you?

Ronnie and dad stood face to face in the middle of the kitchen, Ronnie at 5' 8" was three inches shorter than dad. The rest of us sat on the benches in the kitchen nook. Mom was sitting on her wheelchair beside the potbelly stove. She hated confrontations.

With Judo you grab your stronger opponent by the shoulders, Ronnie said, twist your hips and flip him over your back.

Come on then throw me over your back, dad said.

Ronnie went for dad's shoulders. Dad deflected sideways, grabbed Ronnie by the arms and dumped him at his feet on the floor.

Never underestimate a stronger opponent, dad said, with a smile.

I giggled, dad sat next to me on the nook bench and Ronnie was humiliated, just like I felt when he dumped me on the floor a few weeks earlier.

Since neither you nor Joyce wanted the Doggie Diner, you should get a job, Ronnie, dad said. Don't waste your time with Judo and philosophy and anthropology. You turned down owning my lucrative Diner, so instead you should apprentice as a plumber or an electrician.

Ronnie scoffed at dad's declarations and limped out of the kitchen.

Since Ronnie was twenty-one years old in 1956, he didn't go with us on family outings to Playland or the beach or movies. He was busy with City College courses and his friends, all the while trying to ignore our dad.

Mom was always close to and supported the decisions of her first born. Ronnie didn't resemble the rest of us. His skin tone was darker, his hair black and his face elongated and not round. Whether we had a different father than Ronnie was either a truth or lie and I'd never find out.

ON A SATURDAY that was blistery cold outside I'd stayed inside to watch the old western movie *Stagecoach* on television. The movie starred Claire Trevor, John Wayne, Andy Devine and John Carradine. I'd watched the cinematic movie a couple of times, anticipating the grit of the story. They were all excellent actors and I couldn't wait for the opening scene where the stagecoach came to a dusty halt in Monument Valley to pick up a stranger.

The empty desert, the unhinged sky, the tiny stagecoach and the tall stranger evoked mystery. Unknown to the driver of the stagecoach the stranger was the fugitive named Ringo Kid. John Wayne was the striking young cowboy who vowed to avenge the deaths of his father and brother. Mysteries lay before all the characters in that movie as the mysteries in my family lay before me.

While I waited for the television to warm up, mom and dad were arguing in their bedroom across the hallway, behind their closed door. I rushed to the door and eavesdropped, putting my right ear on the door. I was good at that, exploring and tinkering with the unknown.

A loud statement was made by mom. An equally loud question was asked by dad. Boisterous voices bothered me. Were truths going to be revealed? Energy behind their voices told me yes. Mom was about to reveal a personal detachment and dad had to process her position.

I secretly listened to the wall and took mom's side of the discussion.

He offered me a job, mom said. I need to go to work. The job will help distract from my arthritis.

We have money, dad said. You don't need to go to work.

I'm good with managing money, mom said. The job is part-time and easy. I'll do the gas station accounting four hours a day Monday through Friday.

Benny's still young, dad said. When he comes home from school at lunchtime you need to be here.

I'll work from seven to eleven every day and be home to cook him lunch.

You can't go to work, dad said. We have five kids and I make enough money to support all of us.

Money isn't my concern, mom said. I need a distraction from my condition. The work is just until we leave in June for our trip to Pennsylvania.

I won't have you working, dad said.

The other door from their bedroom to the kitchen opened. I jumped across the hallway into the living not wanting to get caught snooping.

Mom yelled at dad. If you don't let me have that job I'll leave you, goddammit, Mr. Albert Edwin Campbell.

His laughter echoed through the kitchen, through the small bedroom, the short hallway and all the way into his workshop.

Whether mom would leave dad, whether that was the truth or a lie I'd find out soon. Mom couldn't leave dad she was too sick with arthritis and they endured through ample changes and challenges together.

ON TUESDAY May 6, 1956, I remember that date with terrifying intuition. Elvis Presley was going to perform on the Milton Berle television show that evening. Presley's fame was on the verge of gaining international popularity. Karen talked about the handsome rock and roller all week. During school that day I'd asked Jennifer Bell to come home with me so we could watch *Howdy Doody* or some cartoons together on television. That was an innocent invitation to share my family's prosperity. Her family lived six blocks away on London Street in a tiny single-story row house. They didn't own a TV.

Howdy Doody was fun to watch with all the strings attached to his wooden body guiding his actions atop a table. Jennifer and I sat on the floor in front of our television and looked up at the screen. Buffalo Bob Smith directed the action and laughed and joked with the wooden country-bumpkin. Jennifer and I laughed and elbowed each other. Dad stood under the living room doorway, cleared his throat and looked down at Jennifer.

Negroes are not allowed in our home, dad said. You have to leave.

She and I exchanged expressions. Mine was shame. Hers

was fear. Dad exposed his bigotry and Jennifer and I were his casualties.

Jennifer doesn't have a TV, I said. Can't she watch the end of Howdy Doody?

Get out now, dad said.

My friend, eleven-year-old Jennifer jumped up from her cross-legged posture on the floor. Dad stepped aside from the doorway and let her pass through. The front door closed. I dared myself to look dad in his eyes.

Never bring a nigger home again, dad's voice quivered. Do you understand me, Benny?

Yes, I said.

Hot anger shot through my body. I turned back to watching *Howdy Doody*, but the fun I'd had watching the kids program with Jennifer was now malevolent. How could I ever watch Howdy Doody again knowing that dad's racist voice hung in the air?

Dad left the living room while I changed the TV channel. I'd then understood why Jackson, dad's black friend and co-worker at Southern Pacific Rail Road, the mechanic who helped dad repair his cars on our upside driveway, never came inside our house.

I turned off the television, retrieved my toy dump truck and went to the garage to dig for more coins. If I'd give some money to Jennifer maybe she'd forget about what dad said. I knew she wouldn't and hoped she didn't think that I was a racist. Was dad the worst bigot ever? I'd never know the truth. He'd not expressed such an offense again that I'd overheard.

Was our haunted house a problem? Did 402 Avalon make dad bigoted, did the house make everybody laugh at me, did the house make mom a cripple, did the house make Joyce pregnant, did the house make Ronnie hateful, did the house turn Karen villainous, did the house make Timmy accident prone? I'd known that inanimate objects like our house wasn't the offender, but perhaps what had conspired with previous homeowners and tenants, that their spirits were responsible for my family's misfortunes.

My entire family was accident prone.

While in Oroville one summer mom was driving us to

swim in Feather River. The suicide door in the backseat flew open, and when Timmy reached outside to grab the handle and close the door, he was whisked from the car and slammed into a concrete curb. His horrendous concussion took months of recovery. While in Oroville the front tire on Karen's bicycle came off when she was riding it. She flew over the handlebars and smashed her face on the asphalt. Joyce had broken a bone, Ronnie was going to Mexico, mom was almost wheelchair confined and dad, he almost choked to death on a chicken bone.

As for me, well, I'd driven my fist through a window, stepped on a rusty nail and almost killed Bobby Harnwell with rock the size of a golf ball.

The reins of 402 Avalon were wrapped around the Campbell family and tightening. Was the house haunted? Was that the truth or lie? I'd never find out.

More events took place around the neighborhood.

Sixteen-year-old Terry was destined to attend a seminary then become a priest. Our religious neighbor was enjoying himself riding his bicycle around the block that comprised Monroe School and the empty lot. He was strong and loved riding his bicycle. He promised to circle the block ten times. On his fifth attempt up the steep side of Avalon Avenue in the middle of the road, in front of Bobby Elliot's house, Terry dropped sideways off his bike and died from a heart attack. I guessed that God was napping at the time. Was the rumor that Terry had a weak heart the truth or lie? I'd never know.

Truckface, the Campbell Kids Gang name for a local kid, was about to jump over the tall cyclone fence that surrounded Monroe School playground. He grabbed the looped edged on the top of the fence, toed his way up and tossed himself over. The ring on a finger was locked on the top rung and his finger ripped off his hand. He was rushed to a hospital where they were attempting to sew his finger back on. I didn't see Truckface after that accident. If his finger was sutured back on his hand the truth or a lie, I'd never know.

TIME WAS running short in March 1956. Mom was busy

mapping out our round-trip on a large road map of the continental United States. Pennsylvania and New York were far away from California, but we had the entire summer to think about the trip. Perhaps we would visit Yosemite, the Tetons in Wyoming, the Battle of the Little Bighorn in Montana, the windy city of Chicago and when we reached Pennsylvania we could visit Gettysburg where President Lincoln delivered his famous Address. The trip was going to be a reality and mom was busy planning. She'd written down the names of towns and cities where we would stay in motels and special historical sights we would visit along the way. She budgeted for the costs of gasoline, food, motels and emergencies if one or two happened.

If we have enough money left over on the way home we'll swing by Disneyland in Anaheim, mom said to us during one Sunday dinner.

Nothing sounded better to my ears. Disneyland opened on July 17, 1955 and the place would still be new on our return trip in August 1956. Mom seldom teased me so I'd believed that she'd make that happen.

Truth and lies were all-encompassing and at eleven years old I stopped worrying about what truths or lies in our family were about. Five of us lived in the house now. Ronnie was in Mexico City attending the University. Mom helped Joyce move into a studio apartment that had a Murphy bed where she and her new husband slept. Karen, Timmy and I had our own bedrooms, yet I didn't sleep any better than before.

Timmy was fifteen and a solid track athlete as a sophomore at Balboa High School. Karen was thirteen and a poetry writer in the eighth grade and was going to graduate from James Denman Middle School. She started menstruating, and even though Joyce had moved out, I still had to carry two large Tampax packages once a month from Jullianni's store. My embarrassment just wouldn't end.

June was an important date for me, too. I'd be graduating out of the sixth grade at Monroe School without any special interests or skills. Next Fall I'd be attending James Denman Middle School and would then be old enough to evaluate my destiny.

The rumor that dad was going to purchase mom a foreign made compact car was true. Mom was exhausted from driving our big, clunky fastback around the City's crowded streets. The column gear-shift and stiff steering along with the tight clutch made climbing the hills of San Francisco even more challenging. The break petal was big and difficult for mom's tiny foot to push and stop the heavy car. I don't recall if her car was a 1948 or 1949 Plymouth or Dodge or Buick, all I remember is that the car was roomy for us and cumbersome for her to drive.

We'd spent many nights sitting in the backseat of the car at the Geneva Drive-In Theater next to the Cow Palace in Daly City. We'd also spent many hours in the backseat driving to Oroville and back. Dad had what I think was a 1936 Ford Woody. Mom drove the Woody around town when dad wasn't adjusting the brakes and when the engine would start. The steering wheel was huge as were the unsafe bench seats. When we'd hit a pothole or berm in the road my little body would jostle in many directions.

We had so many different cars over a period of five years I didn't memorize the makes and models, but Timmy did. He managed time for memorizing the years, the makes and models of cars. He had a sketch book and would draw futuristic cars that were low to the ground with fins on their backsides. I'd always thought that he'd become a car designer with his obsession for drawing them.

One Saturday morning mom and dad left and said that they were going shopping. Four hours later I was playing in the dirt with my toy plastic army men when mom pulled into the driveway and parked her new gray Renault 4CV beside me. The as-cute-as-a-button French car with the motor in the back with bucket-seats and a stick shift on the floor had me smiling from ear-to-ear, as it did mom. Dad wasn't so impressed when he pulled into the driveway behind her in his what-ever-car he was driving.

The Renault was compact. Four doors made for easy access and exit. Excellent gas mileage would come from the four-cylinder engine and the understated horsepower didn't matter in a city filled with hills. The small size of the Renault made for super easy parking anywhere. All of that was good. But the tires were tiny, the bumpers were flimsy, the headlights were dim, the horn was a toot and those unwise suicide front doors were dangerous, however, the overall cuteness of the Renault diminished everything that it wasn't. There were turning signals on it, rearview mirrors, windshield wipers, and a gearshift stick on the floor and the front bucket seats lent the Renault a spicy individuality. Best of all, the car had that new smell, an odor that appealed to most everybody.

Renault 4CV

You'll never catch me driving that coffin, dad said.

I laughed and the significance of what he said didn't register on me.

Some of our neighbors' interest in her new car had them coming over to inspect the unusual small French automobile, but purchasing one wasn't an option. Neat and tidy and efficient wasn't considered, the car was just too small.

Mom soaked up the Renault's adorability. The car was small and she was small at 5' 2". During the next three months she was happiest when she drove her new fantastic compact car. On weekends she and I drove all over the City, South San Francisco, Daly City, Pacifica and Half Moon Bay. One time she took me to Playland where we purchased enchiladas, a soda for me and coffee for her and she parked the Renault up the road near the Clift House. We ate the delicious enchiladas while looking out over the vast, blue Pacific Ocean. That was when mom revealed something vital to her.

After all those family controversies surfaced over the past two years and most were resolved, one main situation bothered her. She was insecure about herself. She was small and crippled but her personality was large and determined. We lived in a big city filled with criminal activity. With crimes of passion, thievery and murder, crime was nothing new in any growing city. San Francisco wasn't an exception. Worse yet, the Federal Penitentiary Alcatraz was sitting in the middle of San Francisco bay. Nobody had successfully escaped from there, and some of the worst criminals in America had ever known in the past decades were imprisoned there.

Al Capone, Mickey Cohen, Arthur R. "Doc" Barker, James "Whitey" Bulger, and Alvin "Creepy" Karpis, were just a few crazy Americans that suffered the consequences of their crimes by being imprisoned in Alcatraz. Mom's insecurity was legitimate. How could she live in a city filled with crime that bulged with a Federal Penitentiary, or even in an old haunted house on a hillside that had antiquated locks, cracked windows, peculiar foreign tenants, and a history of speculated crimes committed on the premises?

Personal protection for mom escalated, she needed to live in a secure environment and 402 Avalon didn't supply that.

I'm afraid for my life, mom said to me. I can't protect myself so I need a handgun, something small to fit my small hand. A gun that's easy to handle and shoot.

Happiness covered my face. Mom toting a gun around, that would be phenomenal. My mother wanted a gun and I visualized her walking on her crutches with two six-shooters holstered to her hips, something like Annie Oakley, even though that wild-west woman used a .22 caliber rifle for her sharpshooting events in Buffalo Bill's Wild West Show during the late 1880s.

Hey, the 1880s, that was when 402 Avalon Avenue was built.

There's a problem, mom said. I have to get a permit for carrying a concealed handgun and I can't get a permit without knowing how to use a gun.

One-month later mom had a handgun and was I excited. When she showed the firearm to me with the safety on I couldn't believe how small it was. Her palm fit around the handle, her crooked index finger fit seamlessly through the loop and settled on the trigger. Bullets were loaded into a clip that slid inside the bottom of the handle. Considered to be a semi-automatic, a bullet would be loaded into the firing chamber when the gun was cocked by pulling back the topside of the barrel. Should she have educated me about that when I was eleven years old? For my own safety she did, but on the condition that I'd never touch the gun.

If only I could touch the gun. She hid it well, carrying the pistol either in her tiny shoulder holster inside her jacket or behind the sun visor at the top of the windshield in the car. If I'd touch the gun, I'd possibly have killed myself. She'd have killed me anyway if I'd touched it.

Did you get a permit to carry the gun? I'd asked.

I did, she said, and her face lit up. Mr. Cooper's friend took me to a shooting range and instructed me. Applying for and getting the permit was easy, learning how to fire the gun and hit a target is difficult.

I was pretty good at hitting a target bull's eye with my bow and arrow from a lot of practice in Oroville. My wooden pistol whose power was a rubber band and the bullet was a paperclip; I was pretty good at hitting a large target like a car that was driving by while I'd hidden in the tall weeds in the empty lot. Watching cowboys in the movies shoot a gun out of a gunslinger's hand looked easy enough. Could I hit a target using a real gun? I didn't think so and I'd never try to find out.

SINCE MOM had a handgun and a new car, since I had my own bedroom and would be graduating from Monroe School, I thought I should also have a girlfriend. Jennifer Bell wouldn't work because dad said a Negro wasn't allowed in the house. Yvonne wouldn't work because Karen's middle name was Yvonne.

Evelyn Hartung was my perfect choice for a romance.

She was my size and pretty with wavy shoulder-length light brown hair. Bright chocolate eyes, heart-shaped lips, button nose and a delicate chin were features that would make for a beautiful young woman. She was an only child, athletic yet feminine, with slender arms and legs and a clear soft voice. My sixth-grade schoolmate and glee club member, was my perfect choice for a girlfriend, but would she like me?

She would like me. I was the cute little brother of Karen Yvonne Campbell, and if I'd doubt that Evelyn wouldn't like me I'd have Karen stare her down with that wicked, stern expression she was famous for. After Karen's stare Evelyn would have to like me.

Nobody could escape Karen's fabulous yet distressing, terrific yet atrocious stare without giving in to her wishes.

Evelyn and I had already exchanged dreamy glances at each other when I was a glee club member. We'd spoken and swapped pleasantries and even brushed against each other when leaving glee club. Since we had different teachers in different classes, we seldom bumped into each other during recess, so we rarely communicated except for glances at each other down the school hallway or in the crowded school yard.

One Monday afternoon at school she came to me during recess and we stood along the side of the brick building. Our shoulders touched and her eyes sparkled in the sunlight. Her lithe body looked great in the navy-blue dress and black patent leather shoes. She took my left hand in hers and said she had something important to tell me.

Can you meet me after school by the side entrance on Excelsior Avenue?

Can you tell me now? I said.

There isn't time right now, she said. Her touch was soft as she squeezed my hand. I shook my head yes.

The recess bell rang so we mixed with the crowd of kids moving back inside the school, but not without our eyes smiling and drifting over each other. She was sweet and affectionate with me, her smile a lightning rod of appeal, her lingering eyes pools of friendship. After ascending the stairs to the second floor were the six grade classrooms were, we parted in opposite directions down the hallway to our classes.

I sat at my desk trying to read Abraham Lincoln's Gettysburg Address, the entire time thinking pretty Evelyn Hartung had something important to tell me. My imagination kicked in and I couldn't stop it. Did Evelyn want to go steady with me? At eleven years old that was improper. She was so appealing and I knew I was in love with her, well, puppy love anyway. I'd watched scenes in the movies where a young boy and girl were infatuated with each other, but I knew that I'd never let that happen to me.

Maybe Evelyn wanted to marry me. That was ridiculous, only adults exchanged vows of marriage. I put too much emphasis on myself, thinking that our relationship was all about me and I hated narcissism that men so happily endorsed.

The bell sounded and the school day had ended. Kids jumped up from the chairs and raced for the exit. I sat and waited for the room to clear and for my head to clear of speculation of what Evelyn openly wanted to tell me.

Fifteen minutes later, the school yard was vacant except for a couple of janitors cleaning out trash bins. When I set foot outside the side door to the school, Evelyn was waiting for me sitting on the steps. She jumped up and came to me beside the door.

You ruined my afternoon, I said. What's so important?

I'm sorry, she said.

Sadness dripped from her eyes, taking both my hands in hers she squeezed more softly this time. I leaned against the sidewall away from the door. She stepped toward me, puckered her lips and kissed my lips. Warm and soft and dry, that was my first kiss, our first kiss. She backed away and stood beside me. I was confused. She said I'm sorry then kissed me like her kiss was going to be torturous.

We couldn't look at each other and the noise from passing cars in the street and kids laughing and talking when walking and running by us permeated fleeting time.

Evelyn's voice cracked when she spoke. We're moving. My father's job transferred him.

My dazed eyes looked at her. We can still see each other, can't we?

He's transferred to Corpus Christi, Texas. He works for an oil company and they're going to drill for oil in the Gulf of Mexico.

My heart fell to my feet. Evelyn felt my gloom and a small whimper escaped between her lips. She twisted around and stood in front of me. We kissed like adults do in the movies, she put her hands around my neck and I wrapped my arms around her waist. How sweet and delicious she was, but I couldn't think in those terms. As two kids in need of attention we couldn't help ourselves. We'd experienced affection and now we had to break up.

Life was too difficult for two eleven-year old children.

Come to our apartment, she said, we live beside the Granada Theater on Mission Street.

I don't know if I should, I said. Can you bring a boy home?

My parents won't be home until 6 pm after work. Come over and we can exchange phone numbers and addresses.

When are you moving?

She lowered her face and her voice cracked. We're leaving next weekend.

My heart was already resting on top of my feet and now it cracked wide open and started bleeding. I could imagine what Evelyn felt inside. I'd hoped much better than I felt.

Do you love me? Evelyn asked. Her face lit with a wonderful smile and she kissed me on the cheek.

I guess I do, I said. Embarrassment heated up my body and reddened my cheeks. I do, Evelyn, I love you as much as you love me.

She laughed. I didn't say I love you. I'd asked if you love me.

Her teasing was infectious and I pushed her. She pushed me back.

After taking my hand she said, come on, let's go to my place.

Their two-bedroom apartment on the second floor beside the theater was filled with antique furniture and smelled like incense. She showed me around and we settled in for a half-hour at the small dining table where we'd written down each other's phone numbers and addresses. We'd discussed and laughed about how Mr. Howard drilled glee club members into forgetting the words to songs and how devastated I was when he kicked me out of the club.

I should go, I said.

She touched my hand on the table. My parents won't be home for another hour. Can you stay longer?

My mom was expecting me home an hour ago.

She laughed and her eyes sparkled. Call your mom and tell her that you're with me at my apartment and you'll be home in an hour.

You are trouble, I joked. I don't know if I love you.

With saying that I stood up, grabbed the piece of paper with her phone number and address printed on it and headed for the front door. I looked back at her, opened the door and stepped onto the stairway landing. Evelyn followed on my heels, touching my shoulders and pushing me.

I jumped down twelve steps, two steps at a time. Evelyn stood on the landing above watching and laughing. I ran back up the steps and we kissed. She held my hand and wouldn't let go.

I'll see you tomorrow at school? She questioned and freed my hand.

Later alligator, I said, jumping back down the steps.

Stop, she called, just before I opened the door that led to the sidewalk next to the Granada Theater.

What?

Her soft voice echoed down the stairwell. I love you, Benny.

FROM TUESDAY through Friday I walked Evelyn home after school. We'd hold hands standing in the entryway by her front door. Traffic noise and auto exhaust filled the air but silence and stares comprised our conversations. The chilly weather and lack of maturity kept my mind busy, knowing that Evelyn and I had just become friends and our friendship would end as quickly as it had started.

After she'd go inside her apartment stairwell and close the

door behind her, leaving me standing alone, I was primed to perform an experiment that night by calling her every evening before I went to bed to say goodnight. We'd flirt for a half hour. I'd confessed that her touch made my hands sweat and my heart beat fast. She'd replied by saying she loved my brown and green eyes and how innocent they made me look. My experiment that I could still be with her without seeing her had worked.

We said our final goodbye to each other on Friday, a touch of hands and a light kiss was all and she ascended the stairs to her apartment. I scurried one long block up Mission and turned right on Excelsior and went into the sweet-smelling bakery. I'd purchased a strawberry filled doughnut. My life was over and the doughnut filled up the empty space left by Evelyn, but you know, my idealistic longing for living a brilliant childhood had just begun.

The next day, Saturday afternoon I tried to play with my plastic toy army soldiers in the dirt on our upside driveway but my young, shattered heart wouldn't let me. I was a love-sick puppy, but when mom pulled into the driveway steering a blinding fire-engine red and white Ford Station Wagon my love sickness almost vanished.

1956 Ford Station Wagon

Mom stopped and pulled on the handbrake. From the back door that led to dad's workshop I skipped to the car. My mouth hung open in wonderment. The big car looked like a Disneyland fantasy ride. I skipped around the big hunk of red metal, touching the shiny windows, and whisked my dirty finger tips across the glossy paint. The car was wide and long and pretty. Aside from the Renault this Ford was the first new American car my parents purchased.

I opened mom's door and I stood beside her. This is it, Benny, this is our transportation for our trip to Pennsylvania. This will be our home for a couple of months. There's enough room in here for my wheelchair and our luggage.

Mom talking about our upcoming trip didn't make anything sound appealing as much as amplify what the trip would take away from me. Speechless and worried, I ran inside the house, leaped on my bed and buried my face in my pillow. Yesterday I lost my true love and for two months this upcoming summer a station wagon would be my home. Where would I go pee and poop? How would I wash my face and hands and take a bath? How would we cook food and where would we sit down to eat? My life was over and now I'd become a hobo like the men that hung around dad's Doggie Diner.

But that was me. How would Karen, Timmy and mom handle as hobos, living out of a car for two months? Everything at 402 Avalon was changing and I hated the feeling. I felt like I was a hunk of moldable clay and ghost hands were sculpturing my future, and as I listened to conversations and arguments between mom and dad, I knew that the same ghost hands were also sculpturing their futures.

Behind their closed bedroom door, they argued about money and insurance for two new cars, they argued about our dilapidated house and how it was a money pit. They argued about our upcoming summer trip and a job mom wanted to get when we returned.

Mom also declared to dad that she needed to live in a warmer climate to help lessen her arthritic pain and minimize the deformities of her hands, knees and elbows. There was too much pain inside her entire body. There, she told him, she wanted to live in the desert. That was her doctor's suggestion. Nevada, New Mexico, Arizona or Texas, whatever state she lived in didn't matter, as long as she lived in a hot, dry desert climate. Good health and her life depended on living in a hot, dry climate. Dad could request a job transfer from his employer. Southern Pacific Rail Road had rail yards in every major southwest city and dad had the experience and tenure to transfer to any one of them.

We'll see, dad said. Maybe we can buy a house on the peninsula. Buy one of those cracker-box houses that Bertha Webb bought. Live in San Mateo where the weather is warmer.

We can't be copycats, mom said. Besides, that area smells like the dumps.

Was dad softening his attitude, was he kowtowing to his wife and the mother of his children? Did he have a choice not to let his wife have her way? He was the moneymaker, but not the decision maker for the family.

Whether he had an agenda to cover the two months while we traveled was another subject. He'd have 402 Avalon all to himself, not that he spent much time at home, but maybe he would while we traveled. He had plenty of updating and building projects scheduled for the house, and what would he do without a wife and children? He'd revel in his solitude.

Weeks passed by. I think mom told me that any amount of gold can't buy me a minute of time.

January 1956 through April was history and filled with changes. Bobby Harnwell's parents were thinking about selling their house across the street on the corner of Avalon Avenue and Madrid Street. They wanted to move ten blocks up the hill toward McLaren Park and purchase a new house on Gambier Street. The Bertha Webb family had moved down the peninsula to the city of San Mateo. Their new home was inside a gated community, where they'd have better security from the growing crime rate in San Francisco. That didn't mean she wouldn't continue to meet at our house and play cards. Not participating as often is what the move meant. I'd noticed from that time forward only Ann Cram came to play cards with mom.

Neither Ronnie nor Joyce's name were mentioned by any of us, which for me I'd thought was good because they had settled in and were happy wherever they were. May was upon us and June would be the biggest month in my life, the month that Timmy, Karen, mom and I would be packed up in the shiny, new Ford station wagon, pulling out of the upside driveway, headed for parts of the country unknown to me, leaving our past behind. Who knew where we'd end up after so many weeks on the road?

I can't tell you how excited Timmy and Karen were about

our trip, but I can tell you that Karen moped around the house. A change in her body was the culprit. The newness of the red river taking control over her once a month had disadvantages. She was bleeding to death seven days a month and she detested that. The worse part of vacationing for a long time was that mom and Karen would bleed in the car and we had to leave our friends behind for the entire summer.

Mom had made and received several long-distant phone calls during a few weeks. She'd written letters to her father and brothers and Aunt Rose and Albert in Pennsylvania, giving them our visiting itinerary. Travel Checks and cash were secured. The roadmap of the United States was detailed with pencil and red ink marks.

We'd drive a northern route back east and drive a southern route back to San Francisco. Mom scheduled the trip for ten weeks so we'd be back before school started, give or take a few days or another week. The destiny of MinAleta Campbell was calling and she would answer, even if that fate meant dragging her three youngest kids by their ears through hell and back with her.

Just think about the trip, mom said, when we get to Pennsylvania you'll get to meet my father and my brothers and your cousins. You know, Benny, you were two months old when we moved to San Francisco.

I know mom, I said. I should have been born in San Francisco. Do I have to go to Pennsylvania?

THE MONTH of May at school started with our May Day parade party and then a dance in the auditorium. Days prior to the dance, teachers made us practice dancing steps and the boys objected. Who wanted to touch girls, especially putting one hand around their waists in public? I didn't understand the reason for a May Day celebration or the dance, but any type of party festivity was fine with me. At least I got to skip around the maypole like a fairy, squeeze and pop colorful balloons and eat sugar cookies, all because of May 1st.

My most exciting occasion in the middle of the month was

when I marched around Kezar Stadium track with other members of the Monroe Elementary School Crossing Guard Patrol. Twenty-five other guard patrols from schools around the city marched with us in the festivities. If I didn't know better, I'd write that I was in the army because of the extensive military marching drills from the ROTC (Reserve Officers' Training Corps) six weeks prior to the festivities. The training drills were forced upon all crossing guard members at Monroe School. We had to be the best marchers to win the competition. We had to march in perfect unison, turn in perfect unison and salute the officials in unison, and by adhering to the strict rules of command, we'd won the competition. Monroe School Crossing Guards were the best marching guard patrol out of all the elementary schools in the entire city of San Francisco. After being presented the trophy we hollered and tossed our hats overhead.

As much as I enjoyed marching and the adulation from the crowd in the stands admiring and cheering all the little munchkin teams of crossing guards, I'd enjoyed the bus ride with my companions through San Francisco as much. The smell of leather seats in the bus, big windows all around, metal bars to hold onto, the choppy, bumpy streets, and tight twists in the lanes and up and down steep hills, I'd looked forward to that day for three months and the end was upon me, come and gone and I'd have that exquisite memory to recall.

Kezar Stadium

Six grade graduation festivities for me were like trying to remember events in kindergarten class. The kids carried around autograph albums the last week of school, asking classmates, teachers and friends to write short farewell notes, dates and to autograph their page to commemorate their connections. That week passed by like a tornado, blurring all that conspired and much more. I had my small six-by-six-inch autograph album way before graduation and had my girlfriend Evelyn Hartung's signature inside. When graduation came I'd collected many signatures and notes from my friends. Unfortunately, my signature book was discarded, as well as many other memorabilia over the years from that time.

Benny Campbell's sixth grade graduation glass 1956
Monroe Elementary School, San Francisco, California

The morning that our six-grade class photo was to be taken, our teacher assembled us in the hallway on the second floor. We marched like soldiers down the stairs to the first floor and out of Monroe School's large front doors on Lisbon Street. All 29 of us were assembled together by height on one of the two sets of brick stairs. Since I was shy I'd decided that I wanted to be in the last row of kids. This photo shows my face peaking over

Colleen Whiteley's head second to the left in the top row. I ducked down a few inches to prove my shyness.

My last day at Monroe Elementary School was Friday June 8th. As usual, I said so long to a few classmates like that was just another Friday ending the school week. We would reconnect in September when school started for us in the 7th grade at James Denman Middle School at 241 Oneida Avenue, a few blocks on the other side of Mission Street.

At the end of the school day, I walked up to my teacher's desk and we exchange pleasantries. After I was outside of the school on Madrid Street I ran past the empty lot, skipped across the street and opened the door in the fence that led to the garage and into the basement. I started digging up more coins to take on the trip. By saving coins I'd dug up as well as saving my allowance of thirty-five cents a week I'd stored almost twenty dollars. We'd be leaving in a week and if mom needed money to purchase gas during the trip I'd give my twenty dollars to her.

Timmy and Karen were doing the same thing I was doing our last few days at 402 Avalon; telling friends that we would be gone longer this summer because of our six-thousand-mile roundtrip drive.

Pack all your socks and underwear, mom told me. You'll keep your jacket in the car with you. Pack three shirts and three pants.

I only have two pairs of pants, mom.

Pack one and wear one, she said. When we arrive at granddaddy Ben and Marie's house in Butler, I'll wash our laundry there.

What are Karen and Timmy packing?

The same as you, she said. Bring a book and a magazine if you want to read in the car.

When can we go to Disneyland?

That won't be for a few weeks just before we return home.

Over the next three days I packed and repacked my small suitcase. With plenty of room I just didn't know how to arrange my four pairs of socks and three pieces of underwear that would jump around in the big suitcase. My one cowboy shirt, regular shirt and two t-shirts were easy to fold and pack and I didn't worry about wrinkling them.

When you're on the road wrinkled clothes are customary, Karen said.

THE FORD was loaded up. Mom's wheelchair was wobbly in the back of the station wagon on top of our luggage so we could take it out first if she needed it. Timmy sat in the front passenger's side while Karen and I sat in the backseat.

Bobby Harnwell stood in the driveway as did dad, still giving mom directions to call him along the way and when we arrived at Benjamin Larimore's house in Butler. Mom drove the big, shiny Ford station wagon out of the driveway and onto Avalon Avenue, with Bobby and dad waving goodbye.

While gazing back for one last look at the tall, wooden abode that was our home for the last six years, mom turned at the corner of Madrid Street. 402 Avalon had vanished behind us and my brain switched off like somebody had cut the electricity.

Unknown secrets about the history inside our house would remain unknown.

Twenty minutes later we drove across the San Francisco Bay Bridge toward Oakland. The big bridge was my favorite of all because the length of about four and a half miles reached across the wide bay. I could see the bay over the railings and we got to drive through the 540-foot-long Yerba Buena Tunnel that was always filled with traffic reverberations that felt like echoes bouncing in my head.

If shipping freighters were on the bay, I'd see them over the railings. I knew the Bay Bridge well, the east and west entrances and exits and the loud clapping of cars tires on the asphalt, having traveled across the bridge dozens of times over the past five summers going to and from our Oroville shack. I liked driving across the bridge in thick fog that obscured our vision, when we could barely see thirty feet in any one direction, when mysterious feelings of the unknown shot scintillating chills across my skin.

After we crossed the Bay Bridge I curled up and fell asleep.

Traveling

ASSUMING THAT I'd be an unhappy traveler was too noticeable. Before we left the City on the trip, Karen and I were hanging out with each other more frequently. We had a few mutual friends and went to see movies at the Granada Theater together. Sometimes we'd go to bible study together on Sundays at a Baptist church on Ocean Avenue. We'd have uproarious times together at Playland. Timmy was getting a little distant from us because he was getting older and more independent. He'd had a paper route and was taking piano lessons. He also had older teenage friends and activities that excluded his younger sister and brother.

Now all glued together inside the Ford station wagon with no outlet but listening to AM radio stations, and they were few and far between major cities, when reception was scratchy and tinny, we started irritating each other. During antagonizing verbal exchanges between Karen and me the day of the trip, mom yelled at us to settle down. What did it matter if Karen drank more water than me? What did it matter if I had two pieces of chewing gum in my mouth? Our childish behavior did matter if Karen had to open her window after I'd farted.

Settle down goddammit, mom said. Stop arguing, read something and enjoy the trip.

The extraordinary as well as the ordinary aspects about our trip across country now strikes me as comical and tragic, well, not as tragic as in dreadful or disastrous, but as in sad. Mom was crippled and needed a wheelchair and a pair of crutches to walk. She was on a mission dragging us with her. We had to support our physically handicapped mother who was in search for autonomy and who wanted to reconnect to her Pennsylvanian family.

Timmy's interest in cars diverted my attention from Karen for some of the trip. We'd have either died from boredom or have poked each other's eyes out. Kids can withstand watching landscape pass by at fifty-five miles an hour for short periods.

Weeds, agriculture, trees, fences, houses, motels and restaurants all blended together and turned into blurred sequences of ho-hum.

After I'd developed a lack of interest about everything weariness became conventionalized representations of yawning, sleeping, punching Karen on the shoulders, complaining about lack of room, craving to stop to pee then Timmy started counting cars by manufacturer. While mom drove efficiently across two lane blacktops, we counted cars speeding by traveling in the opposite direction.

Fords, Pontiacs, Buicks, an occasional Cadillac and Dodge, Corvette and Thunderbird, and the famous Chevrolet, all were counted by us. Either Ford or Chevrolet had the highest numbers. Bored with that we then counted the colors of cars; black ones, red ones, white ones, blue ones and once in a while a yellow or pink one, we counted all with the interest of mathematics in mind. Yeah, right.

Counting cars didn't save us. We also counted how many clouds were overhead and then we counted people hitch-hiking. Then we looked for shoes, clothing or baggage that was discarded along the roadsides. A lot of junk newspapers and tin cans and Coke bottles littered the roadside soft-shoulders. In distances off the road we saw abandoned and rusted-out cars and trailers, pick-up trucks, clothes washing machines and refrigerators.

Eating food at greasy restaurants, using dirty restaurant bathrooms, stopping at polluted road-side rest stops to sleep, staying two nights in motels, stopping at souvenir stands and surveying junk pieces of pottery, jewelry, miniature knives, forks and spoons engraved with the name of the state, hats and scarves, sandals and moccasins, I decided that I detested that type of traveling.

Did I write moccasins? Timmy, Karen and I had to have leather with leather stitching moccasins that were, by the way, made in the United States of America by Native Indian tribes. Whether those Indians were Arapaho, Cheyenne, Shoshone or Apache, the makers didn't matter to any of us, we just had to wear a pair of real moccasins.

Benny & Timmy in moccasins

Having arrived in eastern Montana at the Battle of the Little Bighorn, the sky was as blue as the ocean and the battle field of Little Bighorn was blanketed with vibrant green summer grass, just tall enough to sway in the direction of the breeze. We jumped out of the station wagon. I had to take a leak without a noticeable public bathroom. I ran over one hillside and did my business all the while thinking I'd get caught but the hillside was vacant. The entire area of rolling-hills was serene as if nothing ever happened there. I zipped up and walked a short distance down the hillside, stopped and viewed the battlefield that once held thousands of Indians slaughtering a few hundred U.S. soldiers and dozens of horses. The absence of the sounds of thundering horse hooves, battle cries and death had me viewing the area filled with melancholy freshness.

After we left Montana we still had to drive through South Dakota, Iowa, Illinois, Indiana, and Ohio and then we'd drive across the border of Pennsylvania. Mom's plan detailed staying at Granddaddy Ben's for a few days then on to Aunt Rose and Albert Smith's to visit with them. After that we'd return to granddaddy Ben's for a few more days or until our welcome wore out.

When we arrived in Illinois and drove through Chicago I was surprised with the cold-blistery late afternoon and how dreary and ugly the city was compared to San Francisco. I'd made a personal note never to return to Chicago much less Illinois.

Driving past green fields and valleys, lakes and small mountains through Ohio and western Pennsylvania mom pulled into Butler, drove around the town by memory from eleven years previous and finally into the long driveway that led to Benjamin and Marie Larimore's home.

Ben's wife Marie, who was mom's step-mom, greeted us with hugs and kisses. She hadn't seen me since I was two months old, or Karen since she was two years old and Timmy since he was four years old. We followed Marie's directions and took turns in the bathroom.

The politics in granddaddy Ben's house had my brain whirling with surprise. The big man of 6', 250 pounds was sitting in his stuffed chair watching a Pittsburgh Pirates baseball game on his television set, disturbing him was tantamount to the 1906 earthquake in San Francisco.

Karen and I walked past the fat man. Hi kids, he said. Don't bother me until the game is over.

After we'd finished using the bathroom we went back into the kitchen. Come here, Marie said. All smiles and hugs, she wrapped her large arms around my shoulders. I just baked apple pie and each of you can have a piece.

Mom entered the house on her crutches, hugged Marie and headed for the bathroom. She walked in front of her dad, they nodded heads after not seeing each other for eleven years, and she went into the bathroom. She knew not to disturb him while he watched a Pirates game.

Set in his ways at sixty-five, he had nothing better to do during his retirement than to mow the several acres of lawn surrounding his house on his motorized lawnmower, watching baseballs games on television and eating. Granddaddy Ben earned his retirement as a lineman for the local power company.

His daughter MinAleta gave birth to six children and his son Howard had one boy and twin girls that were our ages at that time. Many events were part of Benjamin Larimore's life other than eating. He had to mow the lawn, watch more baseball games, hold his twin grandchildren and endure our presence.

Granddaddy Benjamin Larimore mowing his lawn

Mom's dad was aloof to me. My dad and granddaddy Ben had similar attitudes; don't bother me I have a lot on my mind and projects to complete. If you want something, go ask your mother for it.

Granddaddy Ben looked the part of a recluse sitting in his comfortable favorite chair, waited on by his attentive wife and caretaker, happy to see us but unhappy because we had arrived, happy when we left him alone in his living room but unhappy that we'd made too much noise in the kitchen while he was watching a Pittsburgh Pirates baseball game.

He came into the kitchen. How long are you going to stay?

Just a few days, daddy, Marie said.

I'll just close this door so I can hear the game. Don't bother me for about an hour and call me when dinner is ready.

I enjoyed eating my piece of apple pie and watched the big man close the behind him.

In this photograph, and I'm being flippant, you can just see his delight lighting up his face holding onto his twin grandchildren. I should have written; you can just see his grimace, the downturned expression and half-closed eyes like he was in pain. Does granddaddy Ben look familiar to you? I think he'd resembled Oliver Hardy of Laurel and Hardy fame.

After dinner, mom and Marie drank a small glass of sherry

to commemorate hooking up after a decade of separation. Mom never drank because of all the medicine she had to take for her arthritis, yet in our refrigerator back home we always had a bottle of strawberry wine. Dad didn't drink either as a concern of ethics and responsibility. He even gave up smoking cigarettes and cigars.

Granddaddy Ben holding Howard's twins

Whether mom had telephoned dad at Granddaddy Ben's or any other time during our vacation I wasn't aware of it. Mom and dad weren't the best communicators in the universe and as their children, we'd inherited that concept.

Before we went to bed that night, Granddaddy Ben spelled out his commands. Keep the screen door closed. Don't flush the toilet unless you go #2, don't turn on a lamp unless you need the light. Our well water is getting low and electricity cost money. There's enough room for Min and Karen to sleep in the house. How long are you planning on staying here?

That's okay, mom said. Timmy and Benny can sleep on the floor or they can sleep in the back of our station wagon. We'll stay a few days, visit Howard then go visit Rose and Albert. We'll then come back here for two nights then we're off to see Niagara Falls in Buffalo, New York.

We said our goodnights at 9 pm, knowing that we'd have to be up by 7 am for a homemade breakfast of pancakes, eggs, bacon, potatoes and toast. That was way too much food for me.

Timmy and I decided to sleep in the station wagon. The fun

had stopped during the middle of that first night when mosquitos started eating us alive inside the station wagon. We couldn't leave one window open and we couldn't keep one window closed. Either the mosquitos would kill us or the humidity would smother us to death. Our first night's sleep or lack of sleep was torture.

The next day Marie made arrangements with her neighbor for Timmy and me to sleep in their spare bedroom while Mom took us sightseeing through Butler. I think the situation after our second night sleeping at the neighbor's house was that they wanted to be paid per night like a motel. Either that or the wife liked the handsome fifteen-year-old Timmy so much that she wanted to sleep with him.

Neighbors on left side of Marie & Ben

Whatever their argument was about, Timmy and I had to return to sleeping inside the station wagon for a couple of nights until we left to visit our Great Aunt Rose and Great Uncle Albert in the township of Eau Claire. I hated sleeping in the station wagon at Granddaddy Ben's, along with the restricted toilet flushing in the house. The best part for me was meeting my grandparents and sitting on Granddaddy's lawn mower. Marie's delicious meatloaf and mashed potato dinner, then meatloaf and mashed potato left-overs for the next evening's dinner was an amateur chef's dilemma.

At least while in Butler we went to our Uncle Howard's

home, met our three cousins and played badminton all afternoon. Then Uncle Howard lit a barbeque, he and mom visited for a couple of hours, we ate and drove back to Granddaddy Ben's. That was the last time mom would see her older brother, nieces and nephew and the last time Timmy, Karen and I would see our cousins and their dad, Uncle Howard.

Butler, Pennsylvania 1930s-1940s

    The drive to Eau Claire from Butler was less than one hour over narrow country roads, the terrain flourished with lush greenery and trees and not much else. Great Aunt Rose and Great Uncle Albert Smith, the sister and brother who never married, lived in a two-story square craftsman house without the usual big craftsman showcases of porches and awnings, low-pitched gabled roof, wide overhang and exposed roof rafters, yet their abode displayed the simplicity of a true American house that was built during the 1920s and updated throughout the decades.

    Mom pulled our big red and white Ford station wagon over their downward pitched dirt driveway, placing color where brown dirt and the bland gray painted house sat on a slight grade. When I jumped out of the car I surveyed their house. Maintenance was needed. Window frame paint was chipped, the kitchen door screen and doorframe were weathered and splintered, and weeds were spread throughout the yard, something like around our 402 Avalon home. The distant cockeyed barns were on the verge of collapse. We had time-traveled back to the 1920s when epochs of poverty and despair in the United States consumed the country.

How can I explain Rose and Albert's lifestyle without having lived their routines? I will try.

Rose stepped out of the house through the kitchen door, down two concrete-slab steps and greeted us. Medium height and lithe for her sixty something age, Rose's hairdo, dress and shoes were typically 1940s dress code for country women. The pockets in her long white and blue polka dot dress proved that she had crafted it, her big calloused hands and weathered face proved that she worked hard all her life farming the land, milking the cows, slopping the pigs and chasing chickens for dinner, because that's what Rose and Albert did their entire lives, they worked their farm.

Albert plowed the land for growing corn crops, raised pigs, kept horses to pull his rig, shot and killed vermin to protect his crops, raised chickens for eggs and dinner, throw in a cow for milk, a couple of goats for cheese and a handful of feral cats to kill the rats and field mice. This working farm was full of American charm and we city folk were thrown back to an American Pilgrim and Puritan time.

Rose and Albert were subsistence farmers all their lives.

While I was engrossed looking around the property Albert walked up the dirt road from the dilapidated barn and greeted us. Shocking to me was his resemblance to Ray Bolger, the actor who played the scarecrow in the 1939 movie The Wizard of Oz with Judy Garland.

Albert and Rose stood together and Karen snapped their photograph.

Tall and frail with ill-fitting taupe pants and off-white long-sleeve shirt, a V-neck t-shirt underneath his shirt, a tweaked brown fedora hat atop his thin head and giant hands with his thumbs sticking inside his pants pockets and narrow shoulders looking like bookends to his flat chest, Albert Smith was the epitome of a devoted hard-working farmer that ate and drank when he was hungry and thirsty. He was a scarecrow for all I knew, standing beside his house waiving away pesky flies.

I don't recall staying overnight at their home, and yet I do recall eating a scrumptious home cooked meal of creamed corn, beans, corn bread, roast beef and a festive salad. And for a week after that meal, diarrhea proved that I'd chowed downed. I think drinking the raw milk was the culprit.

Rose & Albert Smith, Eau Claire, Pennsylvania 1956

While Rose cooked mom visited with her. Albert took us down to the barn. Karen, Timmy and I chased piglets in the large fenced yard. Fast and slippery the piglets were too sneaky for us to catch. Karen and I stalked at least five feral cats but they didn't want to be seen. The goats scared us with charging expressions in their eyes so we avoided them.

In the afternoon when Rose had our dinner simmering, she took Karen and me down to the barn and taught us how to milk their cow. Wanting to gain a new skill milking the cow I went first, but the big smelly animal objected. Small, cold hands wrapped around her soft, pliable appendages wasn't her choice of friendship, so she kicked my milk can over and swatted my head with her thick, wiry tail. I tried again but got tiny drops of milk. Karen was successful and gathered at least a half-pint in the bucket until Rose took over and milked all four teats until the cow baulked. I carried the milk bucket twenty-five yards up the hill to the house. That reminded me of the gallon water bottles I'd had to carry up the road from the bar-restaurant to our shack in Oroville.

Albert rigged up his horse and one of us snapped his photo sitting on his historic plow. As lifetimes are lived I didn't think that Rose and Albert lived full lives, farming and raising animals for sixty years, but they provided food to their small community of 300, attended church and had friends. Their lives were as full as could be in Eau Claire, Pennsylvania, which was settled in 1848, incorporated in 1900 and comprised a land area of 1.4 square miles.

Albert Smith, Eau Claire, Pennsylvania 1956

When mom and I had visited Rose and Albert again six years later in 1962, they were in their seventies and their living condition was still the same. Albert plowed the fields, raised pigs, killed varmints and harvested corn, while Rose milked the cow, made goat cheese, fixed their meals and washed the laundry. They weren't poverty stricken but had made choices not to venture away from their land and their vocations as farmers. They listened to the radio and didn't own a television. They read newspapers and magazines and socialized with church members but didn't wander away from their roots in Eau Claire.

The brother and sister's house smelled like stale bread and milk. Their hardwood floors were covered with ragged throw carpets, the interior wooden walls were riddled with nail holes from pictures they'd hung throughout the years and, in every room in the house, including the bathroom, hung a head of some sort of animal mounted on wood. Deer with antlers, bobcat, mountain lion, their heads delicately preserved and displayed, and even a full-bodied owl was stuffed and standing on a mount in one bedroom. Heebie-jeebies I felt, and that was an excellent expression that described their house. They were country folk and their simplistic lives reflected that. They grew their own food, raised their own meat, made some of their clothing and stayed healthy and happy, following national and world news via newspaper articles and listening to radio programs.

Leaving Rose and Albert's home was like leaving behind antiquated domesticity as a young adult, disposing the past as history and moving forward into a modern future. Their past was fortified with physical strength and emotional faith, knowing that their lifestyle of subsistence was the backbone of America and not worried about anything outside of their community.

After staying a couple more nights at Granddaddy Ben and Marie's home in Butler our welcome wore out, according to granddaddy Ben. Marie and mom were so close that Marie didn't want us to leave. Her sorrow and pity about mom's arthritis wrinkled her face with worry.

We set off on a new journey to the city of Niagara Falls built along the Niagara Falls waterfalls and the Niagara Gorge, which is located next to the Niagara River that flows from Lake Erie to Lake Ontario.

The drive from Butler to Buffalo, New York, was about four hours, consisting of 200 miles of exceptional scenery over rolling hills and along Lake Erie. The Lake is the fourth largest of the five Great Lakes in North America, with a shore length of about 871 miles and is the recipient of Niagara Falls spillover.

Bundled in my jacket, cotton pants and moccasins, standing with Karen on the concrete overlook area beside Niagara Falls, the mist saturating our clothes, the trudging forces of nature underneath my little feet feeling like earthquake tremors, worried me. Even at my age of eleven I understood that the dynamism of Mother Nature was beyond human restraint, some of nature may be managed but look out, the dangers resembled teenage rebellion when nothing could dominate it.

After Niagara Falls and being on the road for nearly four weeks, I was homesick for San Francisco. Missing Missy and my friends, playing in the empty lot across from 402 Avalon, horseback riding in McLaren Park with Bobby Harnwell, swimming in the YMCA pool with Bobby, riding busses around San Francisco, going for rides with mom in the cute Renault, splurging on rides at Playland, roller-skating and ice-skating, watching movies at the Granada Theater, visiting with my friend Yvonne, playing marbles with James Bell and hopscotch with Rosalie, plus most of all what I'd missed was a delicious salami sandwich on a French roll with a river of mustard from Jullianni's.

The time schedule and with money constraints, eating in restaurants, sleeping in motels, buying gas for the Ford and purchasing small souvenirs along the way, days and weeks that followed remain vague in my memory. Mom drove south through West Virginia, Kentucky then into Tennessee.

Southern United States wasn't my favorite place since I'd heard too many stories back in San Francisco in the news about racial bigotry and hatred coming out of the southern states against Blacks, and that white and black people didn't socialize, had separate neighborhoods, and public facilities and schools, that blacks were less intelligent and lazy. I'd also heard how backward Ozark people were, how incest populated the lowlands and mountain regions, and how because of that, physical abnormalities were common along with mental retardation. Was any of that real?

Alabama proved the reality of bigotry and that continued through Mississippi and Arkansas. We ate in racially separated restaurants, watched white and black folk walk on separate sides of the street. Our time in towns was limited yet we'd witnessed the ignorance and stupidity of social and ethical issues that any intelligent Californian would condemn. As for physical abnormalities and mental retardation amidst southerners, I didn't notice anything different between them and citizens from northern or western states.

Not understanding where my dad's bigotry against blacks came from, after all he was raised in the ethnically liberal state of Pennsylvania, but nevertheless he lived in Caucasian settings in the countryside and schools. I didn't let his racism settle inside me.

WHILE IN the southern states during July the muggy heat zapped my pre-teen energy. I hated summer heat in Oroville and I'd detested hot days driving through Tennessee, Alabama and Mississippi. I tried to keep my car window open while mom drove, hoping the warm wind would dry my sweat. Karen complained the hot wind added to the heat already inside the car. Mother Nature had no mercy in southern states during summers and other seasons brought devastating flooding and tornadoes without pity that destroyed neighborhoods, killed pets and family members.

Like a robot, mom kept driving as though on missions I wasn't aware of. She loved the heat knowing the kindling effects of it soothed and relieved her arthritic pain. She'd drive with her window down, her elbow resting on the car door, the sun burning layers of skin until her eyelids dropped over her eyes. She'd then pull into a roadside rest area and close her eyes. We'd all close our eyes and rest for a couple of hours. Most of the time when I'd awaken from a deep sleep mom was driving again, her window down, just breezing along the highway, looking into the distance for something, anything that would give her comfort for an incomplete life.

In Mississippi one early afternoon, we'd rented a room in a nice motel with a fine swimming pool. We changed into our bathing suits, purchased Cokes and packages of cookies from a vending machine and headed to the pool. Mom joined us for a while then went back to the room to catch a good night's sleep. Beside the pool in the humid, clear sky one-hundred plus heat, Karen fell asleep on a comfortable lounge in her one-piece swimming suit. Timmy and I were busy playing in the pool and forgot about our sister for at least two hours. When I looked at her I laughed. Her face, arms and legs were sun scorched, looking like seared meat on a barbeque. As the recipient of what we suspected to be second degree sunburn, Karen became a verbal, volatile fire-cracker over the next week.

Don't touch me, Karen said over and over. Her face was a red searing torch that could light up a 4th of July celebration. If you touch me, I'll kill you.

Timmy and I would laugh in the car while mom drove. We teased Karen that we'd touch her legs or arms. She'd get vicious and push and punch at us. Mom said she got what she deserved for falling asleep. Was mom like dad; unsympathetic, impersonal, and maybe hardhearted? Yes, she was, and so were we to each other.

Between bathroom stops my stomach growled and my intestines rumbled and snarled. Holding what was inside me was difficult and had to come out immediately.

Benny's farting again, mom, Karen yelled.

You fart, too, mom yelled back.

Several times mom stopped along the edge of the highway, I'd grab a roll of toilet paper, jump out of the car and run for cover, dump my pants to my ankles and squat. That situation wouldn't be anybody's idea of a pleasant vacation or a vacation at all, but there I was squatting red faced and wishing that this vacation was over.

We continued to drive through Louisiana, Arkansas, and Oklahoma and then across the Texas panhandle. The terrain was hopeless, flat, uninteresting and hellish. The weather wasn't even tempting to tolerate. To me the states were lands where people dwelt, biding lives forsaken in hotbeds of hell and not lived lives of excitement. Thinking about running in the cool surf on the Pacific Ocean beach along the Great Highway in San Francisco didn't quite distract me from feeling the stifling temperature we were enveloped in.

I fell short of condemning American citizens for living in the hot states. The cities and towns were their home just like San Francisco was my home, and like them I loved my home even with the shortcomings and uneven social and environmental conditions.

Wherever we stopped, at gas stations, restaurants and motels I couldn't understand the southern accented words people spoke. Southerners on television and in the movies didn't have strong accents like that. I thought their drawls were one big joke and I'd missed the punch line.

Why were we in this godforsaken country anyway? Why did mom take her three youngest children on a lengthy road trip that had turned into arguments then silence between us? Why were we the chosen ones veiled with anger for having to leave our friends and San Francisco behind? Timmy, Karen and I were just beginning our lives back home at 402 Avalon, multiplying our academic knowledge, growing athletic talent, studying and learning about countries and cultures and ethics and discovering points of interest about our personalities.

At eleven years old I knew that mom had dragged us across the country to experience the breadth of the continent and to visit our relatives, but I didn't understand why we had to suffer driving for six, eight or ten weeks eating unfamiliar foods, staying in bug infested motels, tolerating unforgiving heat, sleeping in the cramped station wagon, suffering from diarrhea, sunburn, emotional upheavals, and worst of all, being too young to enjoy myself.

That's what traveling is about, mom said. You'll experience everything, even diarrhea.

Mom had her one intention, and she kept that a secret. Understanding personal secrets, my clandestine effort was about keeping my treasure buried in our garage back home a secret. I couldn't fault mom for confidentiality, although I didn't know about her true motive for another week.

The drive through New Mexico was so otherworldly to me. The stately yet barren and ghostly terrain of plains, mountains, basins, mesas and desert lands disinterested me. Even the swirling sky was a Mickey Mouse Fantasia scene. What was I to do about driving across the state? I would sit and stare and dream about being at Playland across the Great Highway from the refreshing cool Pacific Ocean, riding the roller-coaster, afterward eating a corndog then running with my shoes off through the ocean's surf with Missy.

Across the New Mexico state line was Arizona, another otherworldly, barren and ghostly terrain of plains, mountains, basins, mesas and desert lands. My eleven-year-old brain was singed, and my little eleven-year-old body rebelled. I was a sick puppy, empty of ideas, forsaken as a grain of sand in the

Arizona desert.

Mom's face lit up like a bolt of lightning when she drove into the city limits of Tucson, Arizona. Knowing where she was going, she turned the Ford station wagon on the *Miracle Mile Strip*, the northern segment of Tucson's motel row. Old Pueblo motels shined in the sunlight with swimming pools, flickering neon signs and lush grassy courtyards. Each motel welcomed visitors with names like La Siesta, Wayward Winds, Ghost Ranch, El Rey, Frontier, El Rancho, Riviera, Sunland, Motel El Corral, and thirty more western style motels. All their names blended together as did their lawns, swimming pools, palm trees and communal scorching sun.

She drove up and down *Miracle Mile Strip* until she located the perfect motel to stay at. Was the motel the El Rey or La Siesta, was that the Frontier or Sun Land, was the motel Del Webb's Highway House or Wayward Winds? Since they all looked alike to me, all were insignificant compared to mom's secret.

We'll stay here a few days, mom said. I want to scout around town, see what the University and neighborhoods look like.

We checked into a motel, jumped into our swimsuits and hit the pool. Later that night we thumped into Bob's Big Boy Drive-in on Speedway Boulevard for hamburgers, fries and milkshakes. What better way to introduce us to Tucson, Arizona, than to saturate our palates with fatty foods inside the guise of hell-hot weather.

The hamburgers and milkshakes were reminiscent of the Wagon Wheel restaurant outside of Woodland, on the way to Oroville for summer vacations, where dad and mom would stop and buy hamburgers, fries and milkshakes for all of us. The weather in Woodland was reasonable, not incinerating.

Mom's survey of Tucson and concurrent telephone conversations with dad in phone booths while standing on her crutches, exposed mom's secret, her revelation that she wanted to move to Tucson, the hot, dry desert town, where unrelenting sunshine would almost cure her rheumatoid arthritic condition.

Was I surprised? Hell yeah. I was lassoed, reeled in and tied like a calf in a rodeo and could do nothing to stop the drain of my brain. Karen, Timmy and I didn't even think about calling a meeting to smother mom's dream of moving. Not that revealing our true feelings about a move could change her attitude, but at least maybe how I felt would redirect her emotions.

For the next three days we drove around Tucson, an historic town incorporated in 1877. The population was around 50,000 and growing. The town was modernizing with new neighborhoods and schools. The beautiful brick University of Arizona was where Ronnie could go to school, and Timmy, Karen and I could attend after high school graduation. High school graduation for me was six years away and I knew that mom was hallucinating. Dad's job was in San Francisco, our home was in San Francisco, Karen was going to attend Balboa High School and I was going to attend James Denman Middle School, and that was that.

San Francisco was where we belonged.

Mom knew that and she was in denial.

Tucson is growing by leaps and bounds, mom said. We'll buy a house and Benny can have that 3-speed Schwinn bicycle he's been wanting. And, Mexico is seventy miles south, we could go there and buy sombreros and serapes.

What the hell did growing by leaps and bounds mean? Was that a bribe about the Schwinn bicycle mom hissed into my ears? Who the heck wanted sombreros and serapes? I was a San Franciscan and not a Mexican. We lived in the United States not Mexico. The Mexican person I knew about was the English-mangling Pancho as the sidekick to the Cisco Kid on television. Okay, the duo rode horses around the old west like The Lone Ranger, righting wrongs and fighting injustice wherever they found it, so I'd give them credit for that. But that was the old west and I was part of the new frontier.

Property values are escalating, mom said. We can make money on real estate. There is Davis-Monthan Air Force Base, a Southern Pacific depot exchange that dad could transfer to and the excellent weather that doesn't get too cold in winters or too hot in summers. Tucson is the perfect place to settle down, mom said.

Not too cold and not too hot, perfect! What about the sun

cremating us while walking on the sidewalk? What about scorched lungs and sweltering eyes, what about spontaneous combustion? What about frying eggs on top of the hood of the Ford?

What did we do? When mom drove us to Big Boy's again we drowned our despair by eating more hamburgers and fries—and don't forget about the strawberry and chocolate milkshakes.

By the time we'd get back home at 402 Avalon within a week, I knew that mom would forget about Tucson. I'd raved about James Denman Middle School where my friends and I would reconnect and how I'd continue to buy Tampax packages at Julianni's for her and Karen.

Mom wasn't impressed looking at me with her downturned mouth and scowling eyes.

The next day she drove us to Old Tucson, twenty-nine sizzling switchback miles west of the new Tucson. The searing deserted Old Tucson was a dusty, dilapidated western town built by Columbia Pictures on a Pima County-owned site as a replica of 1860s Tucson, to film the 1939 movie *Arizona*. While mom made me push her around the creepy place, her wheelchair wheels getting stuck on soft sand, with dusty whirlwinds swirling dirt and encrusted muck in our eyes and mouths and hair and ears and nose, mom said: Isn't this great. Fresh air, nature elements, what more can you ask for?

How about a clean Pacific Ocean breeze, mom?

Just get me the hell out of this incinerator, I thought. Mom's elements were opposite of mine. That night I soaked in the bathtub for an hour, trying to scrub Tucson's dirty life off my innocent skin.

Our upcoming Disneyland visit would also be a diversion that would help make mom forget Tucson, and as we drove around the city in its suffocating and unforgiving heat during early august, Tucson wasn't easily forgettable in the eyes of MinAleta Campbell. Tucson was exceptionally memorable for her. I wouldn't let the idea of Tucson change or influence my idealistic longing for living a brilliant childhood in San Francisco. Forgetting about Tucson was equivalent to emotional happiness.

That last night in Tucson I dreamed that I'd missed

listening to the fog horns at night in San Francisco bay, that I'd missed the sound of seagulls screeching overhead at the beach, that I'd missed the silky texture of the misty fog brushing against my cheeks, and how I'd missed watching the fog rolling over Mt. Davidson blanketing the entire valley while the sun hung overhead in the honeyed blue sky. The trolley cars, electric buses, steep streets and Ghirardelli Chocolate, yes, I'd regarded chocolate not as an indulgence, but as a San Francisco paragon of desire, and I'd missed everything, but I'd be home soon to rewire my brain.

Disneyland

MY EXPLANATION for Disneyland in 1956 as an eleven-year-old is that the special place was magical. Disneyland was also fictional yet real, pretend and illusionary, a pipedream come true for Walt Disney. This original play land wasn't just a sudden subculture for children; Disneyland became an extension of culture for artists and scholars, a fantasy world, a developing supernatural, futuristic pop-nation depicting how American society would cultivate a new lifestyle.

The original Disneyland in Anaheim opened with Main Street, U.S.A., Adventureland, Frontierland, Fantasyland, and Tomorrowland on eighty-five acres, each area filled with theme rides and surprises. Disneyland in Anaheim was the only one designed and built under the direct supervision of Walt Disney. His personal dedication was well received nationally:

To all who come to this happy place: Welcome. Disneyland is your land. Here age relives fond memories of the past, and here youth may savor the challenge and promise of the future. Disneyland is dedicated to the ideals, the dreams, and the hard facts that have created America, with the hope that it will be a source of joy and inspiration to all the world.
—Walter E. Disney, July 17, 1955, 4:43 pm—

MOM CHECKED us into a motel. We unpacked and studied the Disneyland grounds map given to us by the motel clerk. We had exhibits to see, circus rides to experience, so many hot dogs and hamburgers to eat and we got started early the next morning.

Mom parked the car and we took turns pushing mom in her wheelchair through the parking lot to the ticket booth. The lanes of entrance were too narrow for a wheelchair so a clerk let us in through a side roped-off entrance. We each received another map of Disneyland. We stepped to the side of Main Street,

U.S.A., where we decided on how to negotiate the ideals, the dreams, and the hard facts that had created America.

This new type of theme park was so cleaver and heartening, with a life-size Mickey and Minnie Mouse, Goofy, Snow White and the Seven Dwarfs prancing back and forth across Main Street that I became dizzy.

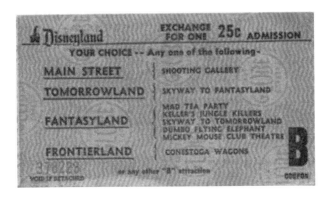

Wanting to go to Tomorrowland would have to wait until I went to Fantasyland and rode the Mad Tea Party and the Dumbo Flying Elephant rides. After I'd ridden those a few times, I needed to see the Rocket to the Moon TWA exhibit in Tomorrowland; after all, I loved space and science fiction movies more than I loved Disney's fantasy characters.

The rides I wanted to take and the exhibits I wanted to see had me following Timmy and Karen walking and running all over Disneyland. For a mapped out plan of discovering the magical theme park, we flew by the seat of our pants while pushing mom in her wheelchair, sweating, out of breath, thirsty and hungry, a little boy without a future, a child wanting, no, a child needing guidance, and what, I was led around an eighty-five acre lot on a hot day, attempting to untangle an entire subculture for children and adults, an older man's pipedream that had admittance fees, and just as inflated were the high prices for food and souvenirs. I was so out of my element that I just wanted to sit and stare at the Sleeping Beauty Castle.

I didn't want the uneasy feeling that I'd missed anything at Disneyland. This important experience for me would prove beneficial. I could brag to my friends and schoolmates that I'd experienced the fabulously new Disneyland, and if I'd overlooked or dismissed any one ride or exhibit, realizing that later would make me miserable. I'd just have to forfeit my carefree youth.

Disneyland 1956

What was my carefree youth? An idealistic longing for living a brilliant childhood while living in San Francisco. After understanding that moving from the diverse city of San Francisco to Tucson, the feelings that I'd be able to create a brilliant adulthood while living in the City would end and that I'd never achieve a dazzling and productive adulthood in the desert town of Tucson.

Karen and Timmy left me behind and headed for Captain Hook's pirate ship, leaving me with mom. I wanted to go on that damn ride with them so I pushed mom too fast in her wheelchair.

Timmy & Karen on Captain Hook's Pirate Ship 1956

Not so fast, Benny, mom said. Put me under the shade tree and go on the ship.

She handed me the camera, Timmy and Karen turned around when I called them and I snapped a photo. I gave the camera back to mom and ran for the cruise on Captain Hook's fabulous pirate ship.

Disneyland represented something more than just a pipedream of a theme park for children and adults. The aspect that Disneyland could be a launching pad for acting and performing careers was plausible. Dancers and singers and actors dressing up in Disney cartoon character outfits then parading around and greeting customers on Main Street, U.S.A. was just a beginning. Who knows what directors and producers would discover them?

I didn't mind all the hoopla surrounding the life-size Disney characters, their comic antics of bowing, taking my hand and dancing and escorting me across Main Street, but a kid can tolerate fifteen seconds of that, and then the thought of punching Goofy in the stomach or kicking Mickey in the shins becomes the norm. Get out of my way and let me enjoy the rides.

What I tried to do at Disneyland for two days was to negate our entire trip and forget about Tucson. I'd set upon a mission of mental destruction by riding as many rides as possible in the shortest amount of time and time was running out.

I pushed mom in her wheelchair following the footsteps of Timmy and Karen. I stopped on Main Street, U.S.A. where one of us snapped a photo of Walt Disney. The fantasy-man was leaning against a short concrete wall between a large poster of Fantasyland and Tomorrowland. That wasn't my concern, I mean guys that looked like Walt Disney was an everyday occurrence. What excited me was that Mr. Disney was conversing with the handsome Paul Newman, I mean he was the guy who starred in the fantastic fantasy movie *The Silver Chalice*, well okay, not so fantastic, but he also starred in the movie *Somebody Up There Likes Me* and that was fantastic.

Paul Newman & Walt Disney

How many people kept a photo of Paul Newman form 1956 when he was fairly new on the acting circuit? Not too many. How many people saved a photo of Walt Disney from 1956? At least I have a photo of Newman and Disney together.

We made a dozen rounds at Disneyland before exhaustion overtook me. My little feet had a couple of blisters from running then stopping, from walking then running, from jumping up and down and swiveling on my toes in moccasins that were now shabby, but there was nothing that a warm shower and a hard night's sleep couldn't cure.

The drive from Anaheim to San Francisco was between five and six hours, give or take an hour or two for pit-stops and eating. Mom was a careful driver yet having to power over the long distance on the infamous U.S. Route 101 or just plain Highway 101 wasn't fun with uncountable thumps in ruts and negotiating dubious repairs, as well as dodging speeding eighteen-wheelers. Driving Highway 101 was like riding a galloping horse in a field full of gopher holes.

Before the Highway Beautification Act was passed in the Senate on September 16, 1965 that called for control of outdoor advertising, including removal of billboard signs along the nation's growing Interstate Highway System and the existing federal-aid primary highway system, except for commercial and industrial zone areas, highway areas were littered with advertising billboards. The act also required certain junkyards along Interstate or primary highways to be removed and the law also encouraged scenic enhancement and roadside development.

Pea Soup Andersen's

As a kid I wasn't concerned with any of that. What I liked were the roadside billboards advertising restaurants, motels and gas stations anywhere from ten to fifteen miles before entering city limits along Highway 101. My all-time favorite was Pea Soup Anderson's billboard.

However, during the drive home I'd slept most of the way jostling on the Ford's back seat with a pillow and jacket and the scratchy Mexican serape I'd purchased at Disneyland. I guessed I'd wanted a serape after all. Karen was sitting beside me sleeping with her head resting on the window. I pulled my feet under me and my moccasins had the beginnings of holes in the soles.

THE SMELL of the San Francisco dumps east of the Southern Pacific railroad in the Brisbane Landfill sifted through my nose. Not often but quite a few times dad used to take us to the dumps with him and that specific acidic odor I knew well.

A couple of times behind his car dad pulled his wooden trailer half-filled with brass and copper piping and fittings. As one of the first recyclers, he'd removed discarded brass and copper from his job at the Southern Pacific Railroad and then sold the metals to the landfill operator by the pound. At the dumps, seagulls would dive-bomb after food scraps and then they'd crap everywhere. The awful garbage smell was so strong I'd pull my shirt up over my nose as a filter. I'd play and search over a dozen large mounds of trash, my shoes sinking in the filth and loving every second, looking for goodies that I could play with, knowing that dad wouldn't let me take anything home.

Mom ignored the dumps and drove toward San Francisco on the US Route 101 Bypass freeway that was also called Bayshore Freeway and/or El Camino Real. The highway was also tagged as *Bloody Bayshore* because the accident rate on Bayshore was twice that of the average California highway, and that included Los Angeles.

The remaining five-minute drive up the slight grade toward Silver Avenue took a lifetime. The smell from the dumps that resembled hardboiled eggs saturated the inside of the car. I opened my window for fresh San Francisco air that was cool to the touch.

My elation experiencing Disneyland had worn off. Our home at 402 Avalon was up the hill. My stomach ached, my head throbbed and I wanted to crawl into my bed and sleep for a week. But now I had that rotten landfill smell imbedded in my clothes and wanted to hurl, but I didn't. I wanted to barf over numerous events about our trip, especially about mom's decision that she wanted, no, that she needed to move to Tucson.

Those thoughts made my body feel nonspecifically wrong with my hyperactive monkey brain dangling in mid-air from segmented feelings.

Late afternoon was misty with the usual low marine layer. Light mist swirled around the Ford station wagon as we drove. Two minutes later Mom turned left off of Silver Avenue and onto Madrid Street. A smile drifted across my lips while looking at the familiar San Franciscan stucco houses along each side of Madrid Street. I'd walked up and down the street past the houses a few hundred times over the past six years with my friends, as well as playing kickball or kick the can in the middle of the street, even roller-skating down the steep sidewalk that always challenged my speedy skills.

My heart pounded when mom accelerated up the hill and out of the mist. One block up the slight grade was 402 Avalon looming on the corner of the block, overlooking the empty lot and the entire neighborhood, like the house was keeping a watchful forbearance across the valley where the top of the cross on Mt. Davidson stood above a blanket of gray fog with celestial blue above.

Mom turned left onto Avalon Avenue, accelerated up the hill forty feet than she turned a sharp right into the upside dirt driveway. Warmth spread over me. I relaxed against my seat and looked out the Ford's window.

Mom turned off the engine, it sputtered for a few seconds then everything went quiet.

Although the big timeworn exterior of the house was a bare tongue and grove dry wooded splintered mess, the mature interior was my home.

Karen and Timmy jumped from the car. After inhaling a couple of times, I sat in the backseat and was dizzy. I'd seen Red Skelton play an intoxicated character many times on his television show so I knew what being drunk looked like, but I wasn't as dizzy inside as I was on the outside.

I jumped out of the car and approached mom's door. She opened it and handed me her crutches. We walked up the long wooden ramp that led to the front door of the house. Dad was at work; the house was cold and Missy stood inside the entryway wagging her furry tail and sneezing repeatedly. That was her usual excited hello.

I fell to my knees and hugged Missy that I'd missed so much. She wiggled and bustled in a circle around me like she'd missed me, too. Mom and dad acquired Missy when I was an infant so we shared the same age, a different species but none-the-less cut from the same era of human/dog friendship. We loved each other and only death would separate us.

Transitions

WE SETTLED in and unpacked. Mom made spaghetti for dinner and afterward all of us went our own way our first evening home. I took a bath, tried to calm my thoughts and before I went to bed I called Bobby Harnwell.

You're finally home, he said. I saw your mom's red station wagon in the driveway.

I pictured him standing in his living room holding the heavy black telephone receiver looking out the window with his parents watching him.

We got stuck in a sand storm in Tucson, I didn't elaborate.

Okay then, see you tomorrow, Bobby said. Wait, was Disneyland fun?

Disneyland was fun, I said, but you know what, not as fun as Playland. All the rides were too far apart and I got stuck pushing mom in her wheelchair through Fantasyland and Tomorrowland. I'll tell you about the rides tomorrow.

Living in limbo at our 402 Avalon haunted house that I loved so much, a few days after arriving home mom and dad had discussed her decision to move the family to Tucson. What family? Timmy, Karen and I were the family.

Mom took us shopping at Sears and purchased three metal travel trunks to pack our clothing in. My own personal trunk was pearly red with a clip-lock and two small keys. I'd rather have had the pirate's trunk in the attic. There had to be some junk inside of it that I could use.

How could we move to Tucson, we didn't have a place to move to? Even though mom told us not to settle in at the house, I'd settled in, reconnected with Richard Patoni and Bobby Harnwell. I was ready to begin my seventh-grade school year. A month until school started would go fast. I was looking forward to attending James Denman Middle School, starting a new social clique, finding skills at eleven years old and locating my place in life. Perhaps even Evelyn Hartung would move back to San Francisco from Corpus Christi, Texas, and we could reconnect.

James Denman Middle School

I was almost at the summit of adolescence when I could loosen up and become an idealistic youth in search of relevance and personal esteem. Life was stripped away from under my feet by mom, as it was stripped out from under Karen and Timmy's feet. They were as frustrated as I was, like three young birds in a nest wanting to fly, and yet none of us could fly-away. Stuck under the wings of our mother we would suffer having to move to Tucson.

Dad took an immediate one-week vacation from Southern Pacific. The next day Mom said we'd be gone for a limited time, to pack a few clothes in paper bags. I called Bobby Harnwell and told him I'd be gone for a few days.

Where to now?

Back to Tucson, I said. Mom wants to move there.

What's wrong with parents, they always want to move, he said. Okay, well, my parents are buying a house up the hill on Gambier Street.

Will you have to go to a different school?

Nah, we're still in the district for James Denman and Balboa.

See you in a few days, Bobby. I hope we don't move away.

WE PACKED enough clothes for one week. The day after that, dad caged Timmy, Karen and I in the backseat of the Ford station wagon with our limited luggage behind us underneath mom's wheelchair. Mom sat in the front passenger's seat.

Dad got behind the steering wheel, started the engine and laughed. We're going for another short fun-filled vacation to Tucson in search for a house to buy, he said.

I was angry. We'd been home a few days and had to hit the road again. This time maybe we wouldn't come back.

You're going to help us choose what house to buy, Dad said.

Like that was a choice he'd let us have.

You're going to like living in Tucson, mom said. The city is growing and there will be more opportunities for all of you. We'll be driving straight through to Tucson over the next twelve hours and we don't want to hear any arguments, complaints or fist fights from the backseat.

We grumbled a little but didn't say anything. I didn't visualize opportunities developing over the years. I just wanted a red Schwinn bicycle and stay living in San Francisco. This move was mom's opportunity to live where she would feel physically better and dad would join us within a year. Moving to Tucson was an excellent choice whether I liked moving there or not.

Dad pulled out of the upside driveway and stepped on the accelerator, driving down Madrid Street he turned right and sped along Silver Avenue headed for the Bayshore Highway. I curled up and fell asleep on the bench seat between Timmy and Karen. They had age-tenure to sit beside the door windows and I was trapped between them for almost nine hundred miles.

Mom had planned convenience stops along the way at roadside rest areas and restaurants. The drive was neither good nor bad, but I was disheveled and irritated, each of us trying to sleep in the cramped backseat, getting stiff necks, backs and legs, and smelling each other's bad breath.

If you have tried to sleep with two other people in the backseat of a 1956 Ford station wagon without touching each other, you'd know what I mean by irritated + annoyed + ruffled + tousled, by the ruffian Karen. She would push and punch and slap and yelp. Don't touch me. Mom, Benny's leaning his smelly body against me. Make him stop.

Stop arguing, mom would yell. Forget about Benny, look out your window and count stars in the sky.

In another month Karen would be fourteen and I'd never seen her so vicious. She'd rather have knocked me out with her fists so I could count the stars in my comatose eyes. Her anger was unrelenting and that squinty-eyed expression didn't cease. The antagonism she presented wasn't temporary either, over the next two years her wrathful resentment about her mother would make her run away twice, hitchhiking back to San Francisco.

After the all-night drive, the next day in Tucson we ate breakfasts at the International House of Pancakes. After noontime we checked in at the same damn motel on *Miracle Mile Strip* in Tucson. The heat was staggering. Fuck Tucson, I hated Tucson, but I didn't think in that expletive, I just hated the incinerating heat that boiled my blood.

After unloading our luggage inside our motel room, we took turns in the bathroom putting on our swimsuits. Timmy, Karen and I darted for the swimming pool. Mom and dad gathered their sweaty selves up and drove down the road to a real estate office.

If we had to be in the intense desert heat, then we had to be in a swimming pool while mom and dad did their house hunting homework. Ideas about why my parents didn't discuss anything with us kids circled in my brain while I splashed cold water over my head. A nebulous thought morphed into maturity; San Francisco was my past and Tucson is my future.

Jesus, why was I even alive?

That night was suffocating, with the screeching swamp air-conditioning unit stuffed in a front window of our room. Water leaked from the backside of the air-conditioner and soaked into the wall beneath. If I'd ever had a nightmare, that was the worst one ever, and that would include the last two years listening to Ronnie's patchy, gruff snoring in the bunk below me at 402 Avalon. Luckily, Timmy, Karen and I had a separate room from mom and dad in the motel. I'd have hated listening to their bickering half the night even though I was awake every minute.

Morning was blinding bright, the sun flaring at 102^0 Fahrenheit by 10 a.m. We'd just eaten breakfast and headed out across Tucson to meet a real estate woman at the first house for sale on the list of three.

The drive across town was intolerable. Wanting to punch myself in the face and knocking my brain to sleep was a thought that popped into my head. If I could run away then all of this would be over but running away wasn't an option. I'd get stung by a scorpion and die. Worse yet, I'd be carried away by a pack of coyotes and become their dinner.

This just wasn't right. Tucson wasn't right for me.

Dad pulled to a curb and stopped in front of a distinguished looking house with tall trees and shrubbery in the yard. The location was a pristine manicured neighborhood. We'd have access to an elite high school, as well as a newly constructed shopping center. Downtown Tucson was a five-minute drive west. After examining three bedrooms and two bathrooms, the elaborate kitchen and large dining room that felt homey, and a cool fenced-in secluded back yard with an emerald green lawn, mom and dad decided the house didn't meet mom's wheelchair requirements; the doorways were too narrow, the main bathroom was too small as was the kitchen and the wall-to-wall carpeting throughout would inhibit easy rolling for the wheelchair.

That was my dream house and they snatched the sweet abode out from under my feet.

Within twenty-five minutes, dad drove to another neighborhood and parked in front of a house to look at, the second house on their list. I don't remember what the neighborhood or the second house looked like because I didn't get out of the car. I didn't care what anything looked like and getting a red Schwinn 3-speed bicycle bribe wasn't worth the move from San Francisco to Tucson. Nothing was worth the move, not even finding a house that could accommodate mom's wheelchair. Not even owning a bicycle that I couldn't ride because the heat would kill me.

The search continued for another two days and all I wanted to do was eat and swim, eat Bob's Big Boy hamburgers and fries, slop down strawberry and vanilla milkshakes, and swim some more, hoping the sun would disappear forever, or at least the weather would cool down from one-hundred ten degrees to a San Francisco degree of sixty-three.

The house search continued for the next two days until mom and dad found the diamond in the rough. Built in 1949, this uncut-diamond was located in the Pueblo Gardens neighborhood. The three-bedroom single-family home at 2143 East 33rd Street was less of a diamond in the rough and more of a stucco nightmare with exterior cracks, a tar and gravel roof and a cement slab for an entry porch. The one bath was sufficient, every room had slick concrete floors for mom's wheelchair, and she could do a wheelchair about-face in the kitchen. With approximately 1,646 square feet, there's an add-on laundry room and best of all there's a large add-on bedroom accessed from the living room. The price of $12,000.00 couldn't be passed up.

2143 East 33rd Street, Tucson, Arizona 1956

That night while eating dinner at some nondescript restaurant with pleasant air-conditioning, thank God, mom explained that Timmy and I would sleep in the add-on bedroom in our new home. The large fifteen-by-twenty-foot room had three windows in the front side of the house and three windows on the side of the house. We would enter the room from the center of one side of the living room that led into a three-foot-wide walk-in closet the width of the bedroom. We'd then step down one step and be in the bedroom. Of course, without an attached bathroom and no heater or air-conditioner, we could leave the screened windows open at night. Wouldn't that be great, windows opened during nighttime?

Just inside the hallway off the living room, Karen's typical bedroom is across the hallway from the bathroom. Mom's bedroom is down the hallway to the right in the back of the house. The bedroom across the hallway from mom's bedroom is Ronnie's bedroom.

Ronnie's bedroom, I said, spewing spaghetti from my mouth. I thought he was going to college in Mexico City?

He is, mom said. We can't afford that any longer so he'll come home here and attend the University. They have an excellent cultural anthropology department.

What's anthropology? I'd asked.

That's Ronnie's course studying the science of humanity.

As he continued his studies I'd have to live with him in a Mickey Mouse house as opposed to our Hearst Castle in San Francisco. The world has ended and I'd be in the desert, sizzling like a hamburger on a grill from the sun, running from killer scorpions and carnivorous coyotes and battling the Attila the Hun Ronnie for my freedom.

There's just one problem, mom said. Pueblo High School and Wakefield Junior High are both three miles away, so you might have to walk to school.

Oh great, now we'd have to walk to and from school, a total of six miles roundtrip, in incinerating heat during September, April and May, and freezing winter weather during October through March. Mom's health may improve but the three of us might get pneumonia and die.

Mom and dad's full price offer for 2143 East 33rd Street was accepted. They signed the papers and after a fifteen-day escrow closing we'd be Arizona residents. I didn't know anything about purchasing a house, much less purchasing an out-of-state house. I felt miniscule like a grain of sand on a beach. The enormity of everything spun my wave of emotions like a top.

We were back at 402 Avalon after another midnight drive

as if we hadn't left San Francisco, as if Tucson wasn't a nightmare, as if my world hadn't spiraled into a nameless, nonentity universe of unknown proportions.

In the top bed of my bunk I lay with ideas spinning a giant spider web around my brain, constricting my thoughts about either running away, or jumping off the Golden Gate Bridge, or lying across Southern Pacific Rail Road tracks, or asking Bobby Harnwell's parents to adopt me. That might be an option and the next day I'd asked Bobby to ask his parents if they'd adopt me.

The next afternoon Bobby and I tossed weed turfs at each other while playing in the empty lot across the street.

My parents won't adopt you, Benny, Bobby said. They don't even want me. But I could see us living together as brothers.

I could sleep in your garage or on your back deck.

Bobby laughed and thumped my head with another wet sod.

DURING THE next month, mom completed moving arrangements by scheduling a large trailer to move household items. Dad would pull the big trailer behind the red Ford station wagon nine hundred miles to our new home in Tucson.

Mon transferred checking and saving accounts with Wells Fargo to their Tucson branch, cleaned out closets in the house, donated items to The Salvation Army, arranged for medical doctor referrals, told Timmy, Karen and I to prepare for the move, all the while dad avoided anything to do with moving to Tucson. He'd moved his young family from Pittsburgh, Pennsylvania to San Francisco eleven years previous and he wasn't participating in another move.

I knew that dad would never move to Tucson and that he and mom were separating. He was a city man with an excellent job and with Mr. Cooper as a business partner. He was also an inventor, an electrician, a carpenter, a plumber, a man of skills, many skills that wouldn't be appreciated or utilized while living in a small township like Tucson. Why would he move to

Tucson? He was fit and handsome, forty-two years old with an economic yet fun personality. He wouldn't move to be with a crippled wife. He wouldn't move to help raise two teenagers and one lonely pre-pubescent son.

In my eyes mom and dad had ended their marriage. Mom had ruined their relationship. Her debilitating rheumatoid arthritis was her internal family that guided her, and Timmy, Karen and I were her mute aides.

My dad to me was a part-time father. I'd see him for short pieces of time on weekends when he wasn't working on his cars in the driveway, or in his workshop designing and making his inventions, and when he wasn't meeting with his partner Mr. Cooper, or napping in his carriage house bedroom, or he wasn't on errands around San Francisco.

All his time would be free after we moved. Whether he would miss me I'd never know. I would miss him though, the musty smell of his clothes, the scent of oil or grease on his hands even though he'd use Borax hand soap to try and scrub off his workday. I would miss his Gilbert Roland smile, his high-pitch laughter, how he'd tell me to respect my mother and help her with the chores. But most of all, I would miss his presence. He was home when he wasn't home, knowing that his clothes, his aftershave, his razor, his sweat-stained hats, his Big-Ben coveralls he'd wear when working on his cars, and every now and then when we'd go out to dinner I would miss him wearing his dark suit and wide red tie with the large blue horsehead printed on it.

Our connection was always about time, not whether he had time for me but if he wanted me around. I'd go to him in his workshop and ask him if I could go to see a movie at the Granada Theater.

Go ask your mother, he'd say.

I already did, I'd say. She told me to ask you.

Dad would pull a $5.00 bill from his pocket and hand it to me.

Here, go to the movie.

The movie costs a quarter, dad.

Keep the five and take some friends. Buy them popcorn and candy. I can't have you around here you might hurt yourself on something.

I know how to use a screwdriver, dad. I won't get hurt.

Go now and see the movie.

Most of the time I wouldn't go to a movie, I'd just hang out in the house, or take Bobby to Baskin-Robbins 31-flavors for a banana split with scoops of vanilla, chocolate and strawberry ice cream served in a row between a split banana. The server would drench chocolate syrup over the ice cream, spread nuts and squirt whipped cream and add a maraschino cherry on top. What better way to saturate my sadness?

What was I going to do in Tucson? I knew what I was going to do. I was going to spend a lot of time helping mom in our new house and missing dad while he lived 900 miles away in San Francisco.

THE TRAILER was in the center of the upside driveway, packed full of furniture and luggage and locked up and ready. Dad hitched the trailer to the Ford then cabled the brake lights to the Ford's wiring.

Missy was beside the Ford waiting for the door to be opened so she could jump onto the backseat. She wagged her tail and was ready to go for a short ride to the Safeway grocery store or even to the beach where she could run on the soft sand and dip into the cold surf. She would never play at the Pacific Ocean beach again. She'd have to gain new skills in the desert defending against killer scorpions, vicious packs of coyote and an occasional carnivorous mountain lion. She had experienced a transgression with a porcupine that stuck her face with a dozen or so barbed quills, which we fixed, but saving her from scorpions, coyotes and mountain lions was danger beyond our control.

According to mom, the one last detail Timmy, Karen and I had to take care of before we drove away from San Francisco had to happen that morning. They had to go to Balboa High School and de-register. I had to go to James Denman Middle School and do the same.

I think we walked together down Avalon Avenue to Mission Street in pleasant cool weather. Mission Street where traffic was heavy but navigable, we walked a few short blocks and turned right and walked down across Alemany Boulevard to Onondaga Avenue where Timmy and Karen went through the entryway into Balboa High School.

I walked another block around Balboa and went into Denman Middle School situated behind Balboa. I know that tears stained my cheeks most of the walk, but that didn't matter because I had to check out of Denman where my friends over the last five years were gathered to further their educations.

I'd never see them again and felt that my education would falter.

At home later, morning before we left I went into the garage under the house and dug up about three dollars of buried coins. The amount of money I'd found didn't matter anymore because my treasure chest was going dry.

I sat back against the mound of dirt and thought about my little Excelsior neighborhood inside the big city of San Francisco.

There would be many hypnotizing features I'd miss not living in San Francisco and my neighborhood. Missing them wasn't because of San Francisco or my neighborhood. I was the cause. I'd become attached to the terrific sights and unique sounds and charming smells that saturated the City and my neighborhood. San Francisco was filled with history and I'd hope I wouldn't forget my past.

My memory was filled with my short history living in our neighborhood. Being a crossing-guard for my school was remarkable, eating salami sandwiches from Julianni's was delicious, sod-fighting and digging tunnels in the empty lot was courageous, the beguiling Campbell Kids Gang was exciting, Judo lessons were challenging and the overall environment was not a dream about life, but reality coming to an end.

Still sitting against the mound of dirt in the garage at 402 Avalon Mom's voice rang out for me to come and get in the car. I'd ignored her beckoning and continued to think about my past.

The history of our house must have equaled that of San Francisco. Apparitions and inexplicable noises throughout the house proved that. Having survived the 1906 earthquake and who knows how many trembling jolts throughout the decades, the foundation and structure was still secure in 1956. Was I scared living in this old house? Sometimes I was nervous, but most of the time I was happy, spirits and all.

I stood up, walked outside and closed and latched the garage doors. Across the street on the upper corner of the empty lot I stood on Madrid Street and Avalon Avenue, musingly regarding the looming old wooden house at 402 Avalon.

My past was breaking the window with my right fist when Timmy and Karen locked me outside. I wore my swim trunks in the bathtub when Timmy and Karen peeked at me through the window over the refrigerator. That and much more was my past.

My past was Ronnie shaking me then throwing me on the floor because I wouldn't tell him where I got the bag of coins; stepping on a rusty nail and having to hold cold hamburger against the injury. And there's more.

My past was watching Missy giving birth to at least six litters of puppies over the years; Timmy slamming his forehead with the heavy lead fishing weight winding around the clothesline wire. And there's more.

My past was watching Karen falling off Monroe School's roof and breaking her arm; Joyce with constant teenage ear infections and coming home late. And there's more.

My past was avoiding mom chasing me around the house on her wheelchair with an extension cord threatening to whip me for not obeying her; sneaking into the attic when forbidden. And there's more.

My past was my secret digging for coins in the garage; throwing a rock and hitting Bobby Harnwell on the forehead. And there's more.

My past was exploring dad's workshop full of tools that could cut off my fingers; dad's singing voice sounding like Nat King Cole; dad always working on something in his workshop; uncountable splinters in my fingers and hands from the rotting railings. And there's more.

My past was setting fire to the kitchen by accident while playing with matches; almost hanging Moosemush from the railing; Puddin' wearing the soles out on her new shoes trying to stop the coaster; walking the upside driveway on stilts dad had made me; setting mouse traps and trapping my own fingers; not knowing one tenant in the apartments on the second floor; having a crush on the young woman tenant living in the studio apartment beside the outside stairway. And there's more.

My past was Mr. Marshall dying in the studio apartment around the back; Bobby Elliot's mother hanging out of her living room window in her house across the street screaming in her scruffy voice for Bobby Elliot to come home for dinner; eating delicious Sunday family dinners mom cooked; eating Chinese food when mom held her card games with Mrs. Webb and Mrs. Cram. And there's more.

Dad taking us to the El Rey Theater on Ocean Avenue to see *Francis the Talking Mule* movies; watching comedy television shows with the family; dreamily observing the giant cross on top of Mt. Davidson, falling in love with Evelyn Hartung, and just living my young life in the haunted ambiance of 402 Avalon Avenue.

Memories of my past bounced inside my eleven-year-old head but didn't trip me up. I'd hoped never to forget any one of my experiences, especially reminiscing about my walk across the street to Monroe Elementary School for six years.

I was privileged to have lived six years at 402 Avalon.

Tucson, September 1956

NOT TALKING for a whole week after arriving in Tucson was agreeable with my new indignant Arizona personality. Outraged, ashamed and scared, but not wrathful, I was just plain resentful with mom and dad for taking me away from San Francisco. I was annoyed with all the people I'd come into contact with at my new school three miles away, Wakefield Junior High School.

Two years later, still resentful and still outraged, I'd received a Certificate of Promotion to High School from Wakefield Junior High School.

> ### Junior High School
> ### Certificate of Promotion
>
> This is to Certify that   ALBERT CAMPBELL
>
> has completed all of the requirements of the course of study for Eighth Grade and is entitled to this Certificate of Promotion to the High School.
>
> Witness our signatures this 29th day of   MAY   19 58
>
> *Frank E. Ott*, Principal
>
> Tucson Public Schools
> Tucson, Arizona
>
> WAKEFIELD Junior High School
> *Robert Dillarrow*, Superintendent

School had already started in Arizona when we arrived in September 1956. The second day after we moved in our new house, Mom took Timmy and Karen to Pueblo High School and registered them. After that she took me to Wakefield and registered me. For that first week she drove us to school until we got our school's bussing schedule. From then forward we took the bus that cost ten cents each way.

Dad stayed with us for two weeks, tweaking the house for mom's wheelchair and installing a fog horn high up on a wall next to the ceiling in the additional bedroom that Timmy and I shared. He wired the horn to an activation button he'd installed in mom's bedroom on the other side of the house. Mom and dad knew Timmy and I wouldn't wake up for school voluntarily, so mom now had a horn she could blast several times when we didn't wake up for school. The intense volume and deep guttural sound from the horn could be heard down the block and the blast would knock us out of bed.

I didn't know how Timmy felt, but I wanted so badly to cut the wires to the horn and stop the madness. All I had to do was get up early enough so that mom wouldn't sound the creepy, alien horn.

Getting acclimated to everything about the desert was difficult; inhaling dusty sand, dried and chapped skin, and that was just during the first week in Tucson. Having horrendous coughing fits from dried-out lungs, experiencing flu like symptoms from the fluctuating hot and cold weather, and that was just the second week in Tucson. Severe headaches came and went, but they stayed and lingered. And that fucking large cacti garden taking up the entire front yard was disgusting. Did I use the F bomb? I did use the F word by that time in my life. My chore was to pull sticker weeds from between the killer cacti, as if getting stuck with the needle-sharp barbs from the cacti wasn't enough torture, I'd now have to pull the fucking weeds that draw blood.

Adjusting to the neighborhood was easy. As the new suburbia, Tucson was still small. Challenging to me was adjusting to the multi-racial students at Wakefield Junior High School. Monroe Elementary School was 99% white, Wakefield Junior High School was 50% Mexican, 30% black and 20% white. Shock and disorientation were the cacophonies that made up my pathway over the next annoying four years.

After a few weeks at Wakefield Junior High I was confronted by a teenage gang and a couple of thugs threatening to beat me up. Thieves and corrupted kids from broken families and teens without fathers filled the classrooms. The teachers keep tight control in the classrooms, but not in the schoolyard, or before and after school. My life was in limbo.

I was on guard and learned how to defend myself in school. The leader of one gang attacked me in the schoolyard while we were playing volleyball. In front of thirty kids I blocked his punches and used Judo to flip him over my back and slammed him on the dirt at my feet.

Thirty kids laughed and pointed at him. That didn't help me.

Humiliated, he jumped up and brushed off his rear. I'll kill you, he said, and left the playground.

I was more frustrated than afraid. I was one innocent kid and there were ten nasty gang members. I spied the hallways for the members. I walked in groups of kids to my next class. I didn't wait alone for the school bus. If I surrounded myself with other kids a gang wouldn't attack me. If one gang member was alone in a hallway he wouldn't bother me, give me the stink-eye, but wouldn't touch me. The Mexican gang members were chickens when one of them was alone and unaided.

My first day in school I'd made one friend named James Willeford and thank God he was honest and clean. He was also big and happy. Twelve years old, six-foot-tall, over the next two years he grew to be six feet two inches and two hundred twenty pounds of muscle. He was my bodyguard since our meeting my first day at Wakefield.

James had a rough life living in a mud hut with dirt floors and with six siblings and no father figure. He didn't want me to come to his home so I'd invited him to our house. We'd decided to assemble a transistor radio together. While he was walking in our neighborhood, just one block from my house, he was arrested by two patrol cops driving by. He was on the wrong side of town, he was the wrong color and he was a threat to the white community. At school I'd apologized and he just laughed, telling me that he was accustomed to being exploited and abused. His fierceness protecting me from a gang carrying knives at Wakefield was appreciated; he'd saved my life several times.

DAD WORKED on the house, making minor plumbing and electrical repairs. Two weeks dissolved and he left to return to San Francisco. He said goodbye without touching or hugs. That was okay by me since we'd never hugged before.

Mom was in heaven. She had relocated successfully to live in the hot, dry desert that she knew would help relieve the debilitating effects of arthritis. Every room in the house accommodated her wheelchair except for my bedroom that was one step down. She had a modern laundry room instead of a ringer-washer and outside cloth line. Setting up doctor appointments to renew her medical prescriptions would happen soon. A grocery store was three long blocks away down Campbell Avenue, wasn't that clever, the Campbell's living one block away from Campbell Avenue.

Downtown Tucson was just three miles from where there's a unique movie theater and charming clothing stores mom could shop at. Ronnie would be returning from Mexico City to 402 Avalon then he would drive the Renault to Tucson, register at the University and sleep in the biggest bedroom in the house.

Everything was hunky-dory.

Karen and Timmy did their best to settle in, but Timmy had similar troubles like me at Pueblo High School with Mexican gangs threatening to beat him up and kill him. Karen cashed in on introversion. Like Timmy and me, Karen didn't like moving from the cool, historic San Francisco, she didn't want to be embedded in a multi-racial school with creepy Mexican and black boys at Pueblo High scamming to get into her pants. She hated everything about hot Tucson and hated everything about crippled mom, and everything about irritating Ronnie. Like me, she wanted to move back to the City that was living in her heart.

September's Indian summer settled upon the desert. I was trying not to settle in the 100^0 degrees suffocating atmosphere. Adding to my confusion was the freaking Davis–Monthan Air Force Training Base less than five miles from our house, where jets pilots would practice breaking the sound barrier at least six times a day. That's the point at which a jet moves from transonic to supersonic speed flying about 768 miles per hour. The ensuing sonic booms felt like war was upon the community. The thunderous velocity of the booms sent surging vibrating waves that shook buildings, shuffled dirt on the ground, and many times unsettled me.

The sound barrier blasts drove Missy crazy. She'd run into our bedroom closet and hide. She was inside the closet most of the time anyway trying to cool off or lying upon the cool concrete floor in the hallway. Missy was bored and listless and a dog friend for her wasn't in sight. Her past was filled with way too many canine followers in the big city and she'd contributed to the dog overpopulation for a few years, but that was history.

I was in Tucson, Arizona, September 1956. Eleven years old, living in a stucco house in the desert, where irritating yelping coyotes sang for a few hours every night, where aggressive killer scorpions wanted to get inside the house and sting me, where jets all day long broke the sound barrier, where gang threats of beating me up hung over me at school, a place that bred depression and survival, a place where dad had deserted us, a place where mom was comfortable with a weary smile that worried me, a place where Missy was depressed, where Ronnie would come to live as an enforcer, a place where I may or may not get a red Schwinn 3-speed bicycle. If I did get one, I'd try to ride it nine hundred miles back to San Francisco. All of that and more happened to me before I was twelve years old.

Into the last week of September, I sat down at our new dining room table with a notepad and pencil and began writing a letter to Bobby Harnwell. My letter went something like this.

Dear Bobby:

    I think using Dear is how a letter is started. I hope you like Denman Middle School. I hate my new school. Six trailer homes are used for classrooms because the regular school is overcrowded with a bunch of nasty kids. There is no air-conditioning in the trailers and I sit and sweat. Going to different rooms with different teachers for each school subject instead of staying in one room with one teacher is silly. I have to take wood-working class and make a coffee table and I hate it. I hate the wood chisels and sanders, drill presses and table saws. School kids here are mean. They push me and kick me and call me white scum. Some boys carry knives and long chains and zip-guns. I hope I don't get killed, but like Karen said, if I don't wake up in the morning don't worry about it.

Is our old wooden house still standing? Did Evelyn Hartung move back? Did you move to Gambier Street? I miss the cool weather. I also miss horseback riding and Playland. I miss riding the bus downtown to Fisherman's Wharf. I miss playing in the empty lot and I miss the spirits in the house. Do you remember the time we played hide-n-seek in the hallway on the second floor when the wall rattled and moved like a wave? Could that have been from an earthquake? I miss looking at the Golden Gate Bridge. I miss the green grass at Golden Gate Park.

Missy hates the desert. Timmy and Karen are in high school. Mom said we'd have to walk three miles to and from school every day. We now ride in school busses instead. I have not seen a rattle snake yet. I've avoided at least six scorpions. There is a thirty-foot-long by twenty-foot-wide cacti garden for a front yard and I have to weed the garden once a week.

Please ask your parents to adopt me. I need to move back to San Francisco. I miss watching the fog roll over Mt. Davidson. I miss everything. I hope I don't die in the desert all alone. I don't want coyotes or mountain lions eating my body or snakes or scorpions making their home under my bones. I'm homesick, Bobby. I'll never be the fun boy I was, enjoying the taste of Ghirardelli chocolate, eating a banana split or enchilada, or cotton candy, or a candied apple at Playland.

If I ever get back to San Francisco will you still be my friend? I'm going to write a letter to Evelyn Hartung. Do you think that is a good idea? Mom looks happy living here. Dad left us and I think I'll never see him again. Could you write to me and tell me if you see him at 402 Avalon. Thank you for being my neighbor. I'm sorry about throwing that rock and hitting you in the head. Tell your parents to adopt me I am sure mom wouldn't mind. I think that we are going to drive to San Francisco next summer to visit my father. I will call you when we get there.

Benny Campbell

I didn't know if I'd finished writing that letter or not. Nonetheless, I'd folded the pages and hoped I didn't misspell any words. I stuffed the two pages in the envelope and wrote Bobby Harnwell's old address of 196 Madrid Street.

TWO WEEKS later after having been punched hard in the back a dozen times and kicked in the rear a couple of times by cowardly Mexican gang members at school, one menacing looking short Mexican kid jabbed his pocket knife at me like he was trying to stab me. After that scary encounter I didn't turn my back on him or any other gang member.

I'd become dehydrated daily from the heat. I'd eat diners consisting of Chef Boyardee canned spaghetti, canned spam sliced and fried, canned spinach, canned corn and canned peas opened and dumped into pans and boiled. Freshly steamed vegetables ended with my life in San Francisco as did Sunday night family dinners. I'd consoled Missy, telling her that life would get better. Mom's fucking foghorn blew my shorts off every morning to wake me up. One afternoon a letter arrived in our mail from Bobby Harnwell.

Excitement is an understatement. I took the letter to my bed, leaned against the wall and with gusto I opened the envelope. Spreading the two pages out in front of me, Bobby's words put me inside a large bubble, where as I read, my new world evaporated, so long, goodbye.

His letter went something like this.

Dear Benny:

You know what you should do about all your problems? Squeal on everybody. You will get beat up anyway. Denman is a long walk from home. I will survive the walking. I like having different teachers and different classrooms. Evelyn Hartung did move back here. I don't know where she lives. You should write her a letter and send it to me. I will give the letter to her at school. You might marry her someday and have kids that look like you.

I saw your dad two days ago. He was with two men dressed in suits. Mr. Cooper was not one of them. They blocked the driveway with six sawhorses. I think that your house will be bulldozed soon. I snuck into your attic last Sunday and took a screwdriver with me. I broke open the lock on the pirate's treasure chest. I hoped there would be gold coins inside. I found twenty-five letters with postmarks dated from 1910 to the 1930s. I tried to read two of them but the words were faded. I think they were love letters. Nothing else was inside the chest so you did not miss much. I heard some spirit voices so I closed the chest and got out of there. I think I saw three invisible men and one woman looking at me. I think I shit my pants so I ran out of the attic. Is your mom going to read this letter? Can I write the word shit?

That was an earthquake on the second floor of your house, when the wall started buckling. Ghosts are just spirits. They are not physical and cannot move material things. You already know that.

We are moving to Gambier Street next month. The walk to Denman will be ten more blocks. I asked my parents to adopt you and they said no. Don't worry about San Francisco. If you move back here someday I will still be your friend. I have not been to Playland or gone horseback riding since you moved. My mother is happy that I do not play in the dirty empty lot anymore. Remember the time you took me to your father's company Christmas party downtown at the

War Memorial Building and I won the drawing for the grand prize of a fifty-dollar gift certificate, and you won a small hand puppet? I'll always remember that, the way the fake Santa pulled on the stupid white beard and bowed on the stage as if all of us believed the hobo was Santa Claus.

You know what? If you come back to San Francisco for a vacation, we can go swimming at the YMCA pool and eat salami sandwiches at Julianni's. My father said that since I do not play much anymore that I am gaining weight. He will play catch with me if I want to. Remember when you beat me up and my mother went to your mother and said that she would not let me play with you anymore? That was one year ago and I still played with you. When you write your letter to Evelyn tell her that you would like to see her when you come here next summer. Ask her for her phone number and address. See, we are still friends because I can give you advice. See you next summer.

Bobby Harnwell

San Francisco Revisited

WHENEVER I'D THINK about San Francisco while living in Tucson, my heart would beat like a jackhammer. A few fascinating structures and landscapes about the City sped through my brain. The most gripping exploration that happened under my little feet was at Playland-at-the Beach.

Mom would take Timmy, Karen and I there a few times throughout the year. Not too often we'd get to take a friend with us, either Bobby Elliot or my friend Bobby Harnwell. The fun at Playland-at-the Beach wasn't just playing inside the Funhouse or riding the roller-coaster, bumper-cars, Ferris-Wheel, but donning ice skates and whipping around the oval track, falling down and skidding on my rear for twenty feet, as well as pulling on my swimsuit and jumping into the freezing Pacific Ocean across the Great Highway. I'd then scarf down cotton candy, hotdogs and hot enchiladas, always my mom's favorite, and sometimes I'd chew on pieces of saltwater taffy.

When I'd feel sick I'd vomited in the bathroom toilet in the Funhouse. That was part of the fun. Feeling the dizzy-headed craziness from the flat spinning turntable, trying to hold on then sliding off and skinning my hands on the hardwood floor and slamming into the padded wall was fun. Climbing up the fifty stairs to the top of the tall metal slide, jumping onto a burlap bag and flying down the fast, bumpy surface and screaming all the way down was deliriously mental. Trying to walk on the moving stairway without falling down, attempting to stand upright all the way through the spinning barrel then falling on my face on the other end before I could get out was torture. Downing sugary junk food ten minutes later and then throwing up amusing chunks of childhood decadence was the end of my day.

The City overall was an excellent adventure for a ten-year-old. Seeing the Golden Gate Bridge up close for the first time was exhilarating. How dazzlingly large and brilliantly designed the bridge was. Construction began January 5, 1933 and was completed on April 19, 1937. It consisted of six lanes, total length is 1.7 miles across, height 746 feet, width 90 feet, and comprised a suspension, truss arch & truss causeways, connecting the northern tip of the San Francisco Peninsula, to Marin County.

Laughing Sal, Playland at the Beach

    Walking across the bridge shrouded in fog, blinded by the ghostly, swirling mist was a world unto itself, the ocean below joined the noise of cars whose spears of headlights and red taillights scintillated images of halos, and yet on clear, windy days the visuals of the water, Alcatraz Island in the distant bay, the City atop hillsides of what looked like whitewashed boxes, all of that contrasted with the blackish greenery of Marin across the bay. That was heaven on earth.

    Although the song *I Left My Heart in San Francisco* was written in 1954 by George Cory and Douglass Cross, Tony Bennett didn't record the song until January 23, 1962, but in 1955-1956 San Francisco was my glorious City-by-the-Bay.

    Officials in many cities had claimed to have their city built on seven hills and the same goes for San Francisco, hills named as: Telegraph Hill, Nob Hill, Russian Hill, Rincon Hill, Mount

Sutro, Twin Peaks and Mount Davidson, but San Francisco had been built on 47 hills.

I'll just reel them off alphabetically: Alamo Heights, Anza Hill, Athens Street, Bernal Heights, Buena Vista Heights, Candlestick Point, Castro Hill (Liberty Hill, Cathedral Hill, City College Hill (Cloud Hill), College Hill (San Francisco), Corona Heights, Dolores Heights, Edgehill Mountain, Excelsior Heights, Forest Hill, Gold Mine Hill (Diamond Heights), Holly Hill, Hunters Point Ridge, Irish Hill, Lafayette Heights, Larsen Peak (Grand View Park), Laurel Hill, Lincoln Heights, Lone Mountain, McLaren Ridge (Shields Orizaba Rocky Outcrop), Mint Hill. Mount Davidson (Miraloma Park * Sherwood Forest, Mount Olympus, Mount Sutro, Mount St. Joseph, Nob Hill, Pacific Heights, Parnassus Heights, Polish Hill, Potrero Hill, Presidio Heights, Red Rock Hill (Diamond Heights), Rincon Hill, Russian Hill, Strawberry Hill (Golden Gate Park, ringed by Stow Lake, Sutro Heights, Tank Hill (Clarendon Heights), Telegraph Hill, Twin Peaks North (Eureka Peak), Twin Peaks South (Noe Peak), University Mound and Washington heights.

At 925 feet Mount Davidson is the tallest, with which the 103-foot tall concrete cross is located.

I was brave enough to travel throughout the City alone on a ten-cent bus ticket with continuous transfers and not tell anybody about my adventures. Mom would take us on exploratory excursion to the Cliff House, Golden Gate Park, Fleishhacker Zoo, Aquatic Park, Fisherman's Wharf, Nob Hill, Telegraph Hill, Twin Peaks, China Town, Marina Green, Lake Merced Park and Civic Center to name a few stimulating locations. My personal excursions were complimentary discoveries that I'd never tell anyone about.

But during my tenth and eleventh years my life was about the old house at 402 Avalon and my family, Monroe Elementary School, and neighborhood friends within a six-block area.

When mom moved us to Tucson my brain stopped working overtime and settled into mediocrity, something of which my sister Karen had experienced and tried to break out of. Neither of us achieved that while living in Tucson for four years.

Would 1957 be a better year for me, when we would visit

San Francisco to see dad and I'd be able to visit my friends and reconnect with Evelyn? I would just have to wait and see next summer.

Campbell Family Photographs

Albert Edwin Campbell
1949 San Francisco

MinAleta Campbell
1956 San Francisco

Ronald Leroy Campbell (Ronnie)
1957 Tucson, Arizona

Joyce Marie Campbell
San Francisco

Timothy Edwin Campbell (Timmy), Karen Yvonne Campbell
1957 Tucson, Arizona

Missy 1957 Tucson, Arizona

Campbell Kids Gang
Timmy, Karen, Benny, Missy
Oroville 1950

Albert Benjamin Campbell (Benny) 1955
402 Avalon Avenue, San Francisco, California

MinAleta Campbell Collage

Al Campbell Collage

Acknowledgements

The advantage of being a writer is that I can communicate my thoughts to readers. Had it not been for the insight of my son Corbett Campbell, 402 Avalon would never have been written. I owe special thanks to my wife Suzy Campbell, for her distinct understanding about my childhood and her perceptive editorial assistance. I give exclusive thanks to Corbett and Suzy, as well as thanks to my family members who had shared my childhood and who in reflection have shared the serious and comedic times with me.

Thank you for taking time to read about some of the zany and peculiar events that ensued during that time of my life. When I was in my late twenties and my son Corbett was five years old, I'd written several children stories that I'd titled Green and Purple Monsters. Their themes challenged senseless bigotry and wrestled with daft ignorance, and I'd written them with my own childhood experiences in mind.

A few years later when Corbett was old enough I'd told him a few stories about my childhood while living at 402 Avalon. We'd laughed at some of the bizarre occurrences, yet the upshot of my stories was that they were real situations. They were actual manifestations of how life was for me and my family back in the 1950s.

Back a dozen years ago, Corbett told me that I should write about my childhood experiences, that I should detail those curious and strange and wacky segments of my life. He was right, I credit him with showering me with the gift to put them in words and bring them back to life, to share with you circumstances that would have been forever forgotten to my family and friends.

Amazon.com paperback and Kindle eBook
ISBN- 978-1490569161 Paperback
ASIN: B00EXAWVK0 eBook

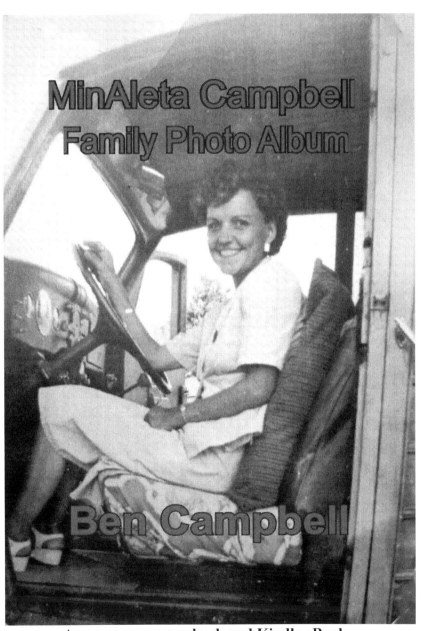

Amazon.com paperback and Kindle eBook
ISBN- 978-1490940915 Paperback
ASIN: B00ESQIAYU eBook

Note Page

Ben Campbell

Ben Campbell is the author of such classic novels as **_KISSINg FREUd_**, **_When Giants Dance_**, **_Dubrovnik_**, **_"Vitruvian Man"_**, **_Regeneration_**, **_Reggie Rocketship and His Galaxy of Secrets_** and **_Marilyn: "It's all make believe, isn't it?"_**, and **_Prettyboy: Fabulous Fifties Hollywood_**. Don't forget about this **_402 Avalon_** memoir and **_MinAleta Family Photo Album_**. They are available as eBooks and paperbacks on amazon.com, Apple iBook store and Barnes & Noble.

Ben grew up in San Francisco, received a degree in Political Science from Cal-State University East Bay. He had worked on a yacht out of Dubrovnik, Croatia, as the U.S. representative to Egypt. He was also an IT Tech at Community Hospital of the Monterey Peninsula. He has published the **_MinAleta Campbell Family Photo Album_** as a follow up to **_402 Avalon_**. He lives in Monterey, California.

Note Page

Made in the USA
San Bernardino, CA
12 January 2019